D1144709

A History of the LMS: The First Years, 1923–30

'Steam Past' Books from Allen & Unwin

THE LIMITED by O. S. Nock
THE BIRTH OF BRITISH RAIL by Michael R. Bonavia
STEAM'S INDIAN SUMMER by George Heiron and Eric Treacy
GRAVEYARD OF STEAM by Brian Handley
PRESERVED STEAM IN BRITAIN by Patrick B. Whitehouse
MEN OF THE GREAT WESTERN by Peter Grafton
TRAVELLING BY TRAIN IN THE EDWARDIAN AGE by Philip Unwin
MAUNSELL'S NELSONS by D. W. Winkworth
MAN OF THE SOUTHERN: JIM EVANS LOOKS BACK by Jim Evans
TRAINS TO NOWHERE: BRITISH STEAM TRAIN ACCIDENTS 1906–1960 by J. A. B. Hamilton
TRAVELLING BY TRAIN IN THE 'TWENTIES AND 'THIRTIES by Philip Unwin
MEN OF THE LNER by Peter Grafton
ON AND OFF THE RAILS by Sir John Elliot
A HISTORY OF THE LNER by Michael R. Bonavia: I. The Early Years, 1923–33
A HISTORY OF THE LMS by O. S. Nock: I. The First Years, 1923–30

STEAM, a year book edited by Roger Crombleholme and Terry Kirtland

A History of the LMS
1. The First Years, 1923-30

O. S. Nock B.Sc., C.Eng., F.I.C.E., F.I.Mech.E.

London
GEORGE ALLEN & UNWIN
Boston   Sydney

First published in 1982
Second impression 1984
Third impression 1984

GEORGE ALLEN & UNWIN LTD
40 Museum Street, London WC1A 1LU

British Library Cataloguing in Publication Data

Nock, O. S.
    A history of the LMS.
Vol. 1: The first years, 1923–1930
1. London, Midland and Scottish Railway –
History
I. Title
385'.0941   HE3020.L75

ISBN 0–04–385087–1

Picture research by Mike Esau

Set in 10 on 12 point Bembo by Nene Phototypesetters Ltd
and printed in Great Britain
by Biddles Ltd, Guildford, Surrey

Contents

Illustrations

Preface

In one of my earlier books, dealing entirely with locomotives, I have referred to the formation of the London Midland and Scottish Railway, on 1 January 1923, as 'the merger nobody wanted'! This is, of course, an over-simplification of a potentially difficult state of affairs. It could scarcely have been otherwise. Historically it cut clean across the policy pursued by the British Parliament from the earliest days of railways, but more remarkably so, it was the only one of the groupings embodied in the Railways Act of 1921 that did so. From the very dawn of main line railways in Great Britain Parliament had set its face resolutely against any form of railway amalgamation that would set up monopolies in definite areas. Lengthwise mergers, notably the London and Birmingham, Grand Junction case of 1846, were accepted, but not those of parallel routes, that would eliminate competition. In 1923 the formation of the London and North Eastern Railway was wholly in tune with age-old precepts. In Southern England the Great Central and the Great Eastern were in no ways competitors with the Great Northern; but it was another matter altogether with the LMS. There was indeed at one time a strong proposal to have a Midland group with a lengthwise merger with the Glasgow and South Western; but this suggestion was eventually dropped.

It was, however, not generally known among members of the public that from a time extending back before the First World War the London and North Western, the Midland, and the Lancashire and Yorkshire had been working in close harmony, eliminating the less important competitive services and introducing many economies. Business-wise it could be said that the major English constituents of the LMS had been 'grouped' for at least a decade before the Geddes scheme was introduced into Parliament, and an alliance between the first, second, and fifth companies of Great Britain, in order of net receipts, would have seemed a very formidable combination. But working agreements, at managerial level, can be a very different thing from full amalgamation.

There had been several pointers as to what might happen sometime before that epoch-marking January of 1923. At the end of 1920 when Sir Thomas Williams retired from the General Managership of the LNWR, to the astonishment of North Western men Arthur Watson, General Manager of the Lancashire and Yorkshire Railway, was appointed to succeed him, while retaining his previous office on the LYR. Then later in 1921 came the news that the latter company was to be absorbed by the LNWR and when this actually took effect, as from January 1922, Watson naturally continued as General Manager of the enlarged company. It was from this time onwards that the upheavals in personnel began, to the dismay of many who had served a lifetime on the old London and North Western. This situation, however, proved no more than a mild foretaste as to what was to happen when the far greater amalgamations of 1923 took place.

It is not the purpose of this book to examine, or criticise the whys and wherefores of the Government grouping scheme that created the London Midland and Scottish Railway. I take it as an accomplished fact, and set down here my impressions of it, as a passenger, a life-long railway enthusiast, an engineer, a contractor, and one who later came to enjoy the privileged position of an observer from the locomotive footplate, from the operating floors of signal-boxes, and the personal friendship of some of its great men. As an author writing about railways generally it was and still, of course, is necessary to maintain a strong degree of impartiality as between the different major administrations; but within the LMS itself, particularly in its early years when partisanship for one or other of the pre-grouping companies was running at astonishingly high level, it is perhaps admissible to let personal feelings intrude just occasionally. So back to New Year's Day 1923.

Twenty Eight   O. S. Nock
High Bannerdown   21 June 1980
Batheaston
Bath

I
Anatomy of a Great Merger

One cannot begin to discuss the formation of the LMS, and all that stemmed from it, without referring back to the momentous amalgamation of a year earlier, which had in many ways altered the entire character of the London and North Western Railway. There is no doubt that the Premier Line had been caught in a weak moment in those first traumatic years after the end of the First World War. It had lost by death and retirement three of its greatest men. It is perhaps idle to speculate how different the course of early LMS history might have been had not Sir Guy Calthrop fallen a victim of the terrible epidemic of influenza that swept the country at the end of the war. He had been no more than forty-four years of age when he was appointed General Manager of the LNWR in October 1914, and, astonishing to recall, he had even then already been General Manager of two major railways, the Caledonian and the Buenos Aires and Pacific. His death, in 1919, was an incalculable loss, not only to the LNWR but to British railways as a whole. Added to that, the retirement, in 1921, of Sir Gilbert Claughton from the Chairmanship, removed one whose strong hand and wise counsel had been invaluable to the railway. The third grievous loss was that of the Chief Mechanical Engineer, C. J. Bowen Cooke, in 1920, one of the greatest locomotive engineers of the day.

It was not surprising, therefore, that when the amalgamation took place in January 1922 with so virile and successful a company as the Lancashire and Yorkshire that men of the latter company took many of the most senior positions. It was galling to men like L. W. Horne, and H. P. M. Beames, who had held such high offices as Superintendent of the Line, and Chief Mechanical Engineer, to be demoted to the position of divisional officers, and this unfortunately was not all. But I must pass on to 1923. The composition of the Board of the LMS, will give some indication as to the way policy became directed in the first few years.

Chairman:
  Hon. C. N. Lawrence (LNWR)
Deputy Chairmen:
  Sir Guy Granet (Midland)
  E. B. Fielden (ex-LYR)
Directors:

W. E. Dorrington	
A. H. Holland-Hibbert	
J. Bruce Ismay	LNWR
G. Macpherson	
Sir Thomas Williams	
W. L. Hichens	
Sir Thomas Royden	LNWR
J. H. Kaye	ex
Sir E. F. Stockton	LYR
G. R. T. Taylor	

Sir J. E. Beale	
Sir A. G. Anderson	
G. Behrens	
C. Booth	Midland
Gen. Sir H. A. Lawrence	
D. Vickers	
A. H. Wiggin	
F. J. Ramsden	Furness
C. Ker	Glasgow & South Western
A. E. Pullar	Highland

1. Sir Guy Granet, General Manager of the Midland Railway and Chairman of the LMS, 1924.

In January 1923 appointments to the Board from the former Caledonian and North Staffordshire Railways had not been made; but under the Railways Act 1921 there remained only five vacancies, because the maximum permitted to the LMS was twenty-eight. Actually, the Caledonian, and to a lesser extent the North Staffordshire, had a long drawn out dispute with the LMS over the terms of amalgamations. The value of the shares, and the apportioning of it into stocks of the new company was generally considered to be made on the basis of the dividends paid on the ordinary shares of the constituent companies in 1913, the last full year before the Government take over of the railways in the wartime emergency. This caught the Caledonian in a weak moment, for their dividend was then only 3½ per cent, compared to the 7 per cent of the LNWR. On this basis they were not to get very good terms in 1923. But the Board argued that their situation had greatly improved since then, and claimed higher proportions. The Caledonian and the LMS reached deadlock in the negotiations, and the case, referred to independent legal arbitration, with some eminent counsel on both sides, was not finally settled until June 1923. In the meantime, at the last Annual General Meeting of the Caledonian Railway Company, in February 1923, the then-Chairman of the company Mr Henry Allan, and Mr William Younger were elected to the LMS Board. A week later Major F. H. Wedgwood was elected as representative of the North Staffordshire Railway. The old companies were therefore represented thus:

14

2. The coat of arms of the LMS.

LNWR, 6; LYR, 6; Midland, 8; Caledonian, 2; G&SWR, 1; Highland, 1; Furness, 1; NSR, 1.

Even so, at the beginning of the grouping era it would have seemed that the dice was loaded against some of the old companies. In the actual process of amalgamation Sir Guy Granet, who had been such a powerful influence in British railway matters since his appointment as General Manager of the Midland, in 1907, was by far the strongest personality in the entire

15

3. A typical Midland goods train passing through the Derby junctions circa 1928, drawn by a Kirtley outside-framed Class '1' 0–6–0 no. 2650 and a standard Class '4F' 0–6–0 no. 4243.

LMS set-up, and it is generally understood that he virtually dictated the general terms of amalgamation.

The chief officers appointed from January 1923 were:

General Manager:	Arthur Watson (LYR)
Deputy General Manager for Scotland:	D. A. Mathieson (CR)
Secretary:	R. C. Irwin (LYR)
Chief General Superintendent:	J. H. Follows (MR)
Chief Goods Manager:	S. H. Hunt (LNWR)
Chief Engineer:	E. F. C. Trench (LNWR)
Chief Mechanical Engineer:	G. Hughes (LYR)
Deputy CME:	Sir Henry Fowler (MR)

The over-riding power in the land, that came to affect working throughout the railway, was the Chief General Superintendent, whose responsibilities were the same as those developed on the Midland Railway, in Sir Guy Granet's time as General Manager, with the dynamic Cecil W. Paget in the key office. Under the new organisation the Chief Goods Manager, who on the old LNWR was generally considered to hold an office that was a stepping stone to the General Managership, was now responsible only for the commercial side of general goods traffic, while the Chief Mechanical Engineer, as on the Midland and the LYR, was not responsible for locomotive running. The newly designated Superintendents of Motive Power were part of the Chief General Superintendent's department. There is no doubt that the operating organisation set up by Paget on the Midland Railway had been outstandingly successful, and during

4. Down excursion passing Kentish Town hauled by
4–2–2 no. 640 and a three-cylinder compound 4–4–0.

the war when Paget himself had taken over command of the Railway Operating Division of the British Army, in France, J. H. Follows had carried on. It was no more than natural that Granet wished to see the same organisation applied to the LMS as a whole, and Follows was the obvious choice for the job.

Of the other chief officers of 1923, Hughes, although the most senior in years and status among the mechanical engineers did not remain in office long enough to have any appreciable influence. It was the Midland faction that came to call the tune, again, of course, with the warm approbation of Sir Guy Granet – for the first

years at any rate. And with Follows and Fowler of more or less the same mind as to how to run trains the Midland influence became, for a time, almost overwhelmingly strong. Although the former LNWR was strongly represented on the civil engineering side with E. F. C. Trench in the chair at Euston since 1909, he represented the old school, when with the title *The* Engineer the office had a degree of omnipotence that even an autocrat like F. W. Webb could not entirely circumvent. On a famous occasion he admitted that he adopted his curious system of 3-cylinder compounding only because the Engineer would not allow him to build his engines wider than a maximum of 8 ft 2 ins, and thus restricted him

17

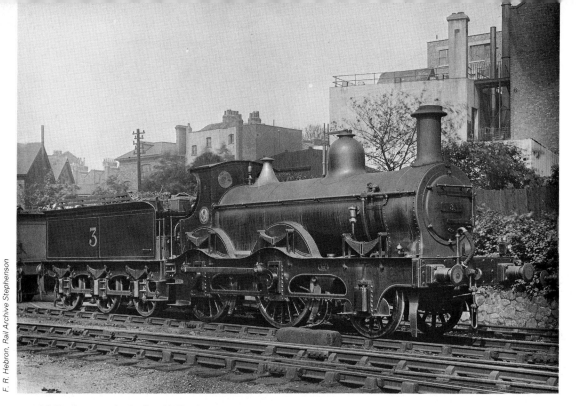

5. A Midland veteran in the first LMS painting style: Kirtley 2–4–0 no. 3 (old 159A, built 1866), at Kentish Town shed on 4 September 1926.

to a maximum diameter of 15 ins for outside cylinders. Trench had certainly allowed Bowen Cooke to go up to 8 ft 9 ins but vetoed the original design of the Claughton class engines, by refusing to agree that the four-cylinder engine layout eliminated the effect of hammer blow on the track.

The parcelling out of the line into separate operating divisions brought some curious anomalies. In the merger between the LNWR and the LYR the enlarged system was divided into Northern and Southern Divisions, with Crewe as the frontier post. The former, including the entire L&Y system, and such important North Western routes as Chester to Holyhead, Crewe to Carlisle, not to mention the maze of LNW lines in Lancashire and Yorkshire, came under a former LYR man,

Ashton Davies. A year later, what became known as the Western Division of the LMS was split into the 'A' and 'B' Divisions, the former including all the former LNWR lines and the latter the former LYR plus the Furness and the Maryport and Carlisle. The Midland Division took in the whole of the former Midland Railway in England and Wales, while the Northern comprised all the former Scottish companies plus the Northern Counties Committee section of the former Midland. The three General Superintendents, each reporting to J. H. Follows were:

Western Division:	Ashton Davies (LYR)
Midland Division:	R. Killin (Caledonian)
Northern Division:	J. Ballantyne (Caledonian)

The appointment of *two* Caledonian officers among the three key operating posts was

6. Coal train, Toton yard to Cricklewood, passing London Road junction, Nottingham, hauled by two Class '3' 0–6–0s.

interesting, and was no doubt indicative of the strong influence of D. A. Mathieson, who had been General Manager of the Caledonian since 1910, and who continued as Deputy General Manager for Scotland, of the LMS until 1927. The pre-grouping railway obviously missing on the operating side of the new organisation was the London and North Western. It was not likely that L. W. Horne, who had been Superintendent of the Line since 1914, and was still a relatively young man, would accept the demotion he received in 1922 with equanimity, and he resigned at the end of the year. The only

North Western man to be appointed as a General Superintendent in 1923 was C. R. Byrom, with the duties of 'Passenger, Commercial' rather than any direct concern with operating. In Scotland, the very distinguished officer who had been General Manager of the Glasgow and South Western Railway since 1894, and had served that railway for no less than fifty-five years, Mr David Cooper, retired, and his going left the way clearer for the subjugation of the 'Sou' West' to Caledonian influences. In England, another retirement was that of Mr Frank Tatlow, General Manager of the Midland, though with Granet and Follows in such commanding positions the precepts of the railway itself were sure to continue.

19

On the locomotive engineering side, in Scotland Pickersgill was almost due for retirement, and although appointed divisional mechanical engineer at St Rollox he did not remain long. At Kilmarnock the stay of Robert Whitelegg was even shorter. He, of course, was a much younger man, and one could not imagine one of his strong character staying in a subordinate position. Within weeks he had obtained the appointment of General Manager of Beyer, Peacock and Co. Ltd, a post that he held with distinction for many years. The only one of the Scottish locomotive engineers to remain was David Urie, of the Highland, a son of R. W. Urie, the Chief Mechanical Engineer of the London and South Western Railway. In England, although Hughes was appointed Chief Mechanical Engineer he was near to retirement, and it was Sir Henry Fowler, who as Deputy CME, was virtually designated as his successor. The man who suffered most severely as a result of the amalgamation was H. P. M. Beames, who had held the full title and status of Chief Mechanical Engineer of the LNWR following the untimely death of C. J. Bowen Cooke. Beames not only suffered demotion, and the subjugation of the great establishment of Crewe, first to Horwich and then to Derby, but had to accept a reduced salary. Whether the rival factions hoped by this graceless act to secure his resignation I do not know; but if so it failed. To his great honour he remained, and by his staunch loyalty to Crewe and to the memory and traditions of the LNWR he rendered an immense service to the LMS, that was to bear fruit richly in the years to come.

On the running side, in the early days of grouping everything was overshadowed by the overwhelming Midland influences that spread throughout the English lines, but which were at first not so strongly felt in Scotland. J. E. Anderson, who had been Deputy CME of the Midland, was appointed Superintendent of Motive Power, and those who knew him often said that he had never been known to speak well of any locomotives except those of the Midland. F. W. Dingley, of the former LNWR, was running superintendent on the lines of his old railway but, of course, completely hamstrung by the new regulations. In Scotland, following the retirement of Pickersgill, W. Barr of the Caledonian assumed command, at any rate everywhere south of the Highland Line. He was a very strong personality, with no exaggerated respect for the newly appointed locomotive authorities south of the Border. I had the pleasure of meeting him years later, when he had retired, and listened enthralled to his reminiscences. Like some of his civil engineering colleagues in Scotland he had his own way of interpreting instructions. As he drily remarked: 'Euston was a long way away!'

On the other hand that very fact was to prove a disadvantage to customers of the LMS in trade and industry who had dealings with what had become outlying areas. The commercial control quickly became a huge centralised bureaucracy, with divisional establishments at Derby, Manchester and Glasgow. Local men who had built up cordial relations and good business with local traders now had to refer to remote centres for authority to arrange deals. There was inevitably delay in getting answers, often hedged around with irrelevant questions and conditions, and it was not surprising that the local people began to seek other means of transport, when they began to realise that under the new organisation their problems were being handled by faraway people who had no knowledge of local conditions. I became particularly aware of what was happening in the Furness district, from which everything had to be referred to Manchester.

2
The Warring Factions

Amalgamations of major business houses, even in the most favourable conditions, are never likely to be times of harmonious settling in, and instant and profitable evolution. From what I have already written, however, it would seem fairly obvious that the scene was set not merely for mild dispute but for implacable confrontation in many areas. The basic organisation alone was anything but generally popular among senior officers, and the choice of men for posts of the highest responsibility sowed the seeds for much friction. But the disputations in high places were nothing to what developed lower down the chains of command, while the loyalties towards the old companies shown by the uniformed staff was a cause of acute embarrassment to management on many occasions. The two principal vendettae were North Western *versus* Midland, and Caledonian *versus* Glasgow and South Western. In the first of these two it was the original and not the enlarged North Western that was primarily involved.

The North Western *versus* Midland clash was made inevitable by the appointment of ex-Midland men to the key operating positions of Chief General Superintendent, and Superintendent of Motive Power. The North Western policy of management had always been to encourage self-reliance and pride in the job among all ranks, and to set store upon a smartness of

manner and appearance, and an innate courtesy in dealing with the travelling public. Back in the nineteenth century the great Chairman, Richard Moon, had impressed upon all his officers the importance of fulfilling what they promised, and that, among other things, meant running punctually to the advertised timetable. This spirit was duly transmitted to all grades concerned with the running of trains. All strove to get there on time, not to greet passengers with a carefully worded apologia as to why they were late!

In 1923 and for some little time afterwards it was no more than natural that the affairs of the locomotive department came under close scrutiny. This was not primarily because it came within the keenest interests of railway enthusiasts, but because of plain economic facts. Of all the different departments on the railway it was by far the biggest spender, and since one of the great advantages of grouping, or so we had been told, was the saving to be realised by standardisation of equipment – particularly in locomotives – everyone from the top management downwards was naturally eager to see what the locomotive department was going to do about it. So far as George Hughes was concerned, with less than three years to go before retirement, it was unlikely that he would be in the mood to initiate any epoch-marking

7. North Western loads, just after grouping: a 'George V' class 4–4–0 no. 2154, 'William Siemens', hauling a train 'equal to 23' (!) at Bushey troughs on 6 August 1926.

reforms, or innovations. He was a man of gentle, almost unassuming disposition, described once to me by a man from one of the smaller railways, who became one of his divisional officers, as 'a dear old man'. His assumption of office on the enlarged LNWR in 1922 had been characterised by a friendly co-operation between Horwich and Crewe, however much the latter establishment felt that somehow it had become the junior partner. It was natural too that Horwich, very proud of its rebuilding of the LYR 4-cylinder 4–6–0s, should want to test them out against their LNWR counterparts, the 'Claughtons'.

Railway enthusiasts of the day were naturally agog to know which was coming off the better, but no details were officially made public. Cecil

J. Allen, as the good journalist he was, sought out the new Horwich engines and wrote of them in a vein that delighted the LYR faction; and some inside information was unofficially 'leaked' to him. As was shown later, however, this gave an impression of these comparative trials which was exactly the opposite of what actually occurred. Only one example of detailed timings on the Crewe–Carlisle road was ever published concerning the dynamometer car tests of 1922. In addition certain features of a south-bound run with an LYR 4–6–0 that were described with a wealth of superlatives, and as something quite novel, I have personally seen surpassed, even in my own then-limited experience of travel, by LNWR 4–6–0s. Horwich had certainly made a good job of rebuilding an early design of Hughes's, which over the years had acquired a really shocking reputation; but as the published results of later tests came to show,

8. The up day Irish Mail near Penmaenmawr in 1924, hauled by 'Renown' class 4–4–0 no. 1968, 'Cumberland' and 4–6–0 no. 233, 'Suvla Bay' ('Prince of Wales' class).

they were considerably heavier coal burners than the Claughtons.

This mild infiltration of Horwich ideas and locomotives was accepted on the old LNWR with a certain amount of amused tolerance, especially when an Aspinall Atlantic was tried between Crewe and Preston. I have no information as to whether this particular test was ever carried northwards to Carlisle. But after the grouping proper, with Anderson taking charge of locomotive running throughout the LMS, and Derby becoming the formidable power behind the benign facade of Hughes's administration, it was no longer a case of gentle infiltration. It was a full-blooded frontal invasion of Midland precepts into workshop practice, running shed working, train loading

regulations and all else. When one considers the record of the locomotive department at Derby over the fifteen years prior to grouping, it seems incredible that such a revolution could ever have happened. On 1 January 1923 Crewe had no less than 505 superheated express passenger engines, any of which could 'lick the proverbial pants' off any Midland passenger engines with the possible exception of the twenty-four superheater 3-cylinder compounds. The latter were limited to a maximum tare load of 230 tons on the fastest trains, so even they, on the face of it, could not be expected to make much of a showing against the 4–4–0s of Crewe, which took 400-ton trains on comparable timings, let alone against the bigger engines.

From the very moment of grouping, however, it was clear that the top-level hierarchy of the LMS was determined to establish a situation of Midland *uber alles*, and the minions of Derby

F. R. Hebron, Rail Archive Stephenson

9: One of the Adams outside-cylinder 4–4–0s of the North London 'stepping it out' through Wood Green with a Broad Street–Potters Bar commuter train.

sailed in everywhere with that object in view. In relation to all on the old LNWR, high as well as low, it was done so tactlessly and so arrogantly as to antagonise everybody. This was nowhere more so than in the matter of train loading. The immediate effect of the imposition of the Midland principles, which had been adopted on the Lancashire and Yorkshire for some time previous to the amalgamation, was to put the former LNWR into very serious difficulties. Under the previous administration, in which the Chief Mechanical Engineer's department at Crewe had the responsibility for locomotive running, those who had the allocation of loco-

motives to duties were given powers of discretion to see that only units in good condition were put onto the most arduous turns. Midland precepts were different. Loading regulations were framed so that a unit in the most run-down condition in which it could still be accepted in traffic could do the job. Thus on trains booked to average 55 mph from St Pancras to Leicester the maximum load for a Midland compound was 230 tons tare, whereas an LNWR George the Fifth class 4–4–0 was expected to take 400 tons tare, and make the same average from Euston to Crewe. The imposition of Midland methods of control immediately made it necessary for many trains on the former LNWR line to be double-headed.

F. R. Hebron, Rail Archive Stephenson

10. An inside-cylinder 4–4–0T of the North London, no. 2874, having discharged its passengers at New Barnet, is working the empty stock forward to Potters Bar and crossing from relief to main line at Greenwood signal box.

But it had some repercussions that surprised the new supervisors. One might have imagined that the enginemen would have welcomed a reduction in the loads they had to take unassisted, which was reduced to 360 tons for *both* classes of superheater 4–6–0, and still less for 4–4–0s; but most of the drivers took it as a reflection on their locomotives and their craftsmanship. A very good story was told some

years ago by T. Lovatt Williams, an old Crewe man, of a driver who we will call Fred, and what happened when he was quizzed by an ex-Midland traffic inspector at Euston. Williams wrote: 'One morning his engine, a George the Fifth was standing at the head of a train in No. 15 platform, Euston, and Fred was leaning over the side of the cab, surveying the scene with a cynical eye. A few minutes before starting time a rather pompous Midland official walked up Platform 15 and counted the coaches as he went along. Thirteen coaches, two

11. Southbound goods on the North Staffordshire line, passing Longport, hauled by ex-NSR 0–6–2T no. 2241.

"diners" – loading equal to "23½". A bit staggered by this he walked up to Fred and said: "Good morning, driver, where's your pilot engine?" Fred looked him up and down, removed the dreadful old pipe from beneath his straggling moustache and remarked: "In the shed, where she ought to be. Who do you think we are, the b——— Midland."'

Actually '23½' would have been two eight-wheelers over the old North Western limit; but to take two extra coaches, if need be, was quite in the spirit of the old LNWR. The opinion of the men was not improved when the first trials of Midland engines on the two-hour Euston–Birmingham expresses began towards the end of 1923. On those trains the George the Fifth class 4–4–0s had been rostered to take loads up to 350 tons tare, without a pilot, at which everyone on the Midland was horrified. In the first wave of infiltration, however, the climax was reached when Anderson thought he could work the lighter two-hour trains with Midland

12. Evening Furness-line express leaving Carnforth for Whitehaven. The last two vehicles are ex-LNWR through from Euston. The engine 4–6–4 no. 11101 is painted in Midland red.

Class 2 superheater 4–4–0s. Engine no. 557 was brought over for the purpose together with her a well-known Kentish Town driver. Cecil J. Allen reported, however, that it 'had to be worked very hard to maintain time, and was withdrawn after a somewhat serious mishap.' What the mishap was did not get disclosed, but a month later he published details of a run on the 4.50 pm up from Birmingham, on which the load was the derisory one, for the North Western, of four coaches and a dining car – equal to '8' by the old reckoning. Allen had previously recorded in the *Railway Magazine* time-keeping with such a load by a 2–4–0 Precedent class engine. To set the Midland Class 2 performance on record, unique so far as I know, the log is appended.

LMS 4.50 pm BIRMINGHAM–WILLESDEN JUNCTION

Load: 160 tons tare, 170 tons full
Engine: ex. MR 4–4–0 No. 557

Dist Miles		Actual m s	Speeds mph
0.0	BIRMINGHAM (NEW ST)	0 00	—
3.8	Stechford	5 22	—
10.1	Hampton-in-Arden	11 17	68/58
18.9	COVENTRY	19 35	75
—		sigs	
30.3	RUGBY	31 45	37
37.6	Welton	40 30	
43.2	Weedon	45 25	72
53.0	Roade	54 15	60
58.1	Castlethorpe	58 35	74
66.2	BLETCHLEY	65 52	64
72.7	Leighton Buzzard	72 04	61
81.2	Tring	80 58	52
95.4	WATFORD JUNC	94 47	—
107.5	WILLESDEN JUNC	107 45	—

27

Schedule was then 109 minutes, which may be compared with the 107 minutes of 'Special Limit' timings on the Midland over the 99.1 miles from Leicester to St Pancras. On that timing the load for a Class 2 engine was 180 tons; but it must be remembered that Class 2 included the various non-superheated rebuilds of the Johnson 4–4–0 engines, both with 6 ft 6 ins and 7 ft coupled wheels.

The different attitudes towards locomotives on the major English constituents of the LMS were wittily summed up by D. W. Sandford, engineer in charge of testing at Derby, and one of the few Midland men of the day who was willing to crack a joke at the expense of his old company. In a discussion at the Institution of Locomotive Engineers on post-grouping policy he said: 'At Derby the nice little engines were made pets of. They were housed in nice clean sheds, and were very lightly loaded. There must have been a Royal Society for the Prevention of Cruelty to Engines in existence. At Horwich they had gone all scientific and talked in "thous" though apparently some of their work was to the nearest half-inch. At Crewe they just didn't care so long as their engines could roar and rattle along with a good paying load, which they usually did.'

I would not like to think anyone reading this chapter might imagine I have an anti-Midland bias. I was at school within sight of the Midland Railway in the north country for five years, and grew as fond of that great line as I am of any other; but what made my hackles rise at the time, and still does, as I learn more and more of what went on behind the scenes in those first years of grouping, was the way in which its precepts were steam-rollered across those of other great and hitherto-prosperous railways, regardless of the circumstances. That the London and North Western interests and great potentialities did not become completely submerged and eventually sunk without trace was in very large measure due to the stout-heartedness of H. P. M. Beames at Crewe, who, despite shabby treatment amounting almost to professional insult, still kept the flag flying; and as I shall tell in a later chapter did a great job of modernisation in Crewe Works.

3
The Scottish Situation: More Midlandisation

In reflecting upon the relatively sparse Scottish representation on the LMS Board, only four seats out of a total of twenty-six, this was in some way related to the capital investment in the pre-grouping companies. Looking at the situation as it was just before the First World War, in round figures the capital of the eight companies represented on the Board, in millions, was London and North Western, 120; Lancashire and Yorkshire, 72; Midland, 160; Furness, 7; North Staffordshire, 9; Caledonian, 46; Glasgow and South Western, 19; Highland, 7¼. In relation to the investment the representation of both the Caledonian and the Glasgow and South Western was low, but in actual working the appointment of so able an engineer and administrator as D. A. Mathieson as Deputy General Manager for Scotland ensured that Scottish interests were not swamped, in favour of the far greater investment south of the Border. As long previously as 1899 he had been appointed Engineer-in-Chief of the Caledonian and in 1910 he had succeeded Guy Calthrop as General Manager. With the retirement of David Cooper from the Glasgow and South Western at the time of grouping, Mathieson was by far the most senior in office of all the general managers

of the constituent companies of the LMS, Watson of the Lancashire and Yorkshire having succeeded Sir John Aspinall as recently then as 1919.

I travelled north of the Border for the first time in the early autumn of 1923, and there was then no sign that any changes were taking place. Caledonian and Glasgow and South Western locomotives were still confined to their original systems, and all still in their original colours. I saw a number of Caledonian engines that had recently been through the shops for general overhaul, including one of the two original McIntosh express passenger 4–6–0s, no. 50, and they looked magnificent in the blue livery. The only evidence of the new order was that Highland engines of the Clan class were working through between Inverness and Glasgow (Buchanan Street). The last four engines of that class were painted in a lighter shade of green, and superbly clean they made a striking contrast to the blue Caledonians, in Buchanan Street station, and at Balornock shed where they stayed overnight. So far as the locomotive management was concerned Pickersgill seems to have dropped out of the picture almost at once, and Barr's strong hand took his place.

13. A great G&SW veteran: a 7-ft 4–4–0 of James Stirling's 1873 class, as rebuilt with Smellie-type boiler and Manson cab; in Midland red and numbered 14236.

This was to have some repercussions later; but within a year there were some important changes on the operating side.

The original organisation of the Chief General Superintendent's department as described in Chapter 1, did not last long. C. R. Byrom, previously General Superintendent (Passenger Commercial), was appointed Assistant Chief General Superintendent, and with this appointment it was apparently not considered necessary to have separate assistants dealing with the Western and Midland Divisions. Ashton Davies took Byrom's previous job, and

R. Killin returned to Scotland as General Superintendent (Northern Division). J. Ballantyne, the first holder of this latter office, was appointed Goods Manager for the Northern Division. An interesting development, however, was that the Northern Counties Committee section of the former Midland Railway, in Northern Ireland, was placed under the Northern, and not the Midland Division. This was a logical move, because the NCC lines, by the Stranraer–Larne sea route, were more closely associated, traffic wise, with Scotland. As matters developed some of the most distinguished officers of the NCC came from Scotland. It was in 1924 that the man who galvanised the NCC into one of the most

14. One of the celebrated 'Skye-bogies' of the Highland Railway, originally no. 7 built 1898, here seen at Dingwall, in Midland red, numbered 14284.

efficient of all sections of the LMS, Major Malcolm S. Speir, was appointed Assistant General Superintendent, Glasgow.

From the very moment the constitution of the LMS was announced it was evident that the choice of a standard livery for locomotives and coaching stock would prove a thorny question, and one that, however decided, could not give general satisfaction. One could hardly imagine a more diverse, or individually distinguished collection of passenger locomotive liveries, than those sported by the constituent companies: 'blackberry black', Midland red, and Caley

blue, would have been enough in themselves; but then add the greens of the G&SW and the Highland, the striking iron-ore red of the Furness, the madder-brown of the North Staffordshire, and the near-malachite green of the Maryport and Carlisle! The most impartial way out would have been to choose a colour different from all of them; but impartiality was not the mood of the top management of the LMS in 1923–4, and almost needless to say they decreed it should be Midland red. To Crewe this was just the last straw, but strangely enough, although in Scotland it signified the loss of an outstanding, and much cherished mark of individuality – particularly on the Caledonian – it was received with considerably more equanimity

31

15. Two contrasting Caledonian 0–4–4Ts of Dugald Drummond's 1886 class. The leading one, no. 15103, has just been repainted in Midland red; the other, in 'Caley blue', has become rather shabby.

than on the LNWR. When the Highland engines were decked in the new colours they were kept most regally clean.

On the Clyde the pleasure steamer fleets of the Caledonian and G&SW Railways were amalgamated, and for the very first season of grouping all the ships had the new style of colour code for the funnels. Previously, the Caledonian Steam Packet Company had yellow funnels, without any black cap at the top, while the G&SW had red funnels with a black cap. Old travellers on the Clyde did not approve of the hybrid, compromise style of funnel, with a black cap, yellow at the base and a red band intervening; but one could still distinguish between ships of Caledonian and G&SW origin,

apart of course, from the names. The former retained their black hulls, while those of the G&SW remained light grey. There is little doubt that the ships of the old 'Sou-West' were among the most handsome and most favoured of any on the Clyde, though the paddle box decorations on the Caledonians, were of a beauty and elegance scarcely believable today. In 1923, when I first sailed in the Clyde steamers the services were still precisely those of the original companies. The process of paring down one-time competitive services had not begun.

In England the first steps towards the Midland philosophy of operation began to take shape on the former LNWR lines. The aim was to provide a frequent service of relatively light trains, as on the Midland itself, rather than the intermittent service, often loading up to massive tonnages that had always been characteristic of the North Western. Furthermore the strict

16. The magnificent arched roof of Glasgow St Enoch, now demolished, dwarfs the Manson 4–4–0 no. 14176, heading a train of six-wheeled coaches on 11 June 1927. Note the Caledonian type of semaphore route indicator in front of the chimney.

limitation of loads, to suit the available motive power on the Midland, made it generally desirable to aim at load standardisation, and avoid the necessity of strengthening coach formations at times of maximum traffic. The up Scotch Express leaving Leeds at 5.15 pm by which I made a number of runs, provides an interesting example. It carried portions from both Edinburgh and Glasgow, and I travelled on it at both holiday peaks, and between times. Its minimum load was about 230 tons tare, but once after Christmas, and again towards the end of the Scottish tourist season the loads were 267 and 301 tons tare, both absolutely packed with passengers, and in the latter case double headed, with a Class 2 superheater piloting a compound.

By way of contrast the 10 am down Scottish express from Euston, which was divided into separate Glasgow and Edinburgh sections from Crewe, and each attaching through portions from Birmingham, provided an equally interesting example of the way the North Western dealt with peak traffic. The Glasgow portion had a minimum basic formation of only six coaches, a five-coach dining car set from Euston, and the one coach from Birmingham. Yet as traffic built up a separate dining car was included in the Birmingham section, and I have known the train made up to *fourteen* vehicles leaving Crewe. Yet with ample engine power in the form of a 4-cylinder Claughton class 4–6–0 no piloting was necessary, even over Shap. This kind of practice cut clean across Midland ideas of operating, and one of the first significant moves was to try to cut down train loads. On some services Midland coaches were substituted for

33

17. An immaculate HR 4–4–0 no. 14384, 'Loch Laggan', on a Blair Atholl to Perth train at Pitlochry: note the Midland six-wheeled clerestory van next to the engine.

North Western, because they provided equal seating accommodation for a smaller tare weight, but in many cases this did not avoid the widespread piloting that had become necessary from the greatly reduced maximum loads laid down for the North Western 4–6–0s. Following the alleged superiority of the Hughes 4–6–0s over the Claughtons consequent upon the trials made in 1922, construction of many more was authorised: an additional thirteen by the end of that year, and another twenty-two were built at Horwich in 1923. A final twenty followed in

1924–5; but although many of these were put on the Crewe–Carlisle road they were subjected to the same load limits as the Claughtons.

In the first phase of Midlandisation on the English lines of the LMS serious consideration was given to recasting the entire service over the former LNWR system; to operate it with a swarm of frequent, lightly loaded express trains any of which could be run by a locomotive of Class 4 capacity. The application of the Midland system of power classification was another sore point. At the time details were published the technical basis of the classification was also made public; but to all of us who had made a close study of locomotive capacity on the solid grounds of actual performance on the road, the

18. One of the Pickersgill 'Oban-Bogie' 4–6–0s, no. 14619, on an up train near Taynuilt.

results, whatever their technical basis seemed materially at fault. So far as LNWR locomotives were concerned, the superheated Precursors, Experiments and George the Fifth class engines were all in Class 3, along with the Johnson Belpaires of the Midland, and all the Caledonian superheater 4–4–0s. In Scotland the allocation of the Pickersgill 3-cylinder 4–6–0s of the 956 class to class 5 was a travesty of their ability. In actual performance they would have been hard put to equal an average Class 3 4–4–0!

Locomotives and train working apart, however, in the New Year's Honours List of 1924 Arthur Watson, the General Manager, was knighted, though on the grounds of ill-health he retired almost at once, and was succeeded by his deputy, the Rt Hon. H. G. Burgess, PC. Watson's retirement, and Burgess's appointment, moreover, coincided with the retirement of Lord Lawrence of Kingsgate from the chairmanship of the company, and the election to succeed him of Sir Guy Granet. Although it could be thought that the Midland grip on the top management of the company was thereby strengthened, and was to be still more so in just over a year's time when George Hughes retired, and Sir Henry Fowler became Chief Mechanical Engineer, the new General Manager, formerly with the LNWR, brought a leavening of immense experience, in very different fields, and undoubtedly helped to pave the way for the radical changes in organisation that were to follow in a few years time.

Burgess was a member of a well-known Tipperary family, and for over twenty years before the war served as Irish Traffic Manager, including in his duties the Managing Directorship of the Dundalk, Newry and Greenore Railway. He was also for sixteen years a director of the Dublin and South Eastern Railway, and for four years of that period Deputy Chairman. In 1917 he became Director of Transportation of cross-Channel traffic between Ireland and Great Britain, and also acted as the representative of the Coal Controller (Sir Guy Calthrop) in Ireland. In 1919 he resigned his various railway offices in consequence of being appointed to Government office as Director of Irish Transport in the Ministry of Transport. He returned to the LNWR in 1920, as Principal Assistant to the General Manager, then Sir Thomas Williams, a post later designated as Deputy General Manager. At the time of the merger between the LNWR and the LYR, Burgess had been in the railway service for more than forty-eight years, and could well have looked forward to retirement, or at least to some lessening of responsibilities; but he continued as deputy to Watson, and then carried on in the supreme executive office during the vital formative years when the entirely new organisation was being evolved, under the skilful and discerning hand of the new Chairman, Sir Guy Granet.

4
Locomotives: The First Four Years

The appointment of J. E. Anderson, formerly Deputy Chief Mechanical Engineer of the Midland Railway as Superintendent of Motive Power for the entire LMS system – who until the fateful autumn of 1926 had never been heard to speak well of any engine, save those of Midland design – led to a sustained attempt to prove that the Midland compounds were the most suitable for standardisation on an all-line basis. It was the first time the locomotive men of Derby had had access to a dynamometer car, and it was natural, while George Hughes was still in the chair, that the former Lancashire and Yorkshire vehicle should have been preferred to that of Crewe. Hitherto Midland locomotive testing, no more comprehensive than the taking of indicator diagrams, had been carried out mainly from Derby, on the heavily graded route to Manchester, over the Peak; but now that the Midland engines were to be brought into direct competition with their rivals from other constituents of the LMS the Leeds–Carlisle line was chosen.

The first set of trials, which began on 10 December 1923, were made entirely with Class 4 locomotives: a standard superheated compound against one of the equally rated 999 class

19. Sir Henry Fowler, Chief Mechanical Engineer of the LMS, 1925–1930.

37

20. Ex-LNWR 'Prince of Wales' class 4–6–0 in the first LMS painting style.

simple 4–4–0s, and a London and North Western 4–6–0 of the Prince of Wales class. None of the Scottish locomotives included in Class 4, the Caledonian Cardeans and Pickersgill 60 class 4–6–0s, nor the Highland Clans and Rivers were sufficiently numerous to be considered as a possible future standard. So far as the actual trials were concerned, it can be said that never before had there been such hard running on the Midland Railway. The timings of the Scotch Expresses between Leeds and Carlisle came within the 'limited load' category, on which the maximum unpiloted load for a

Class 4 engine was 260 tons. The test trains were first made up to 300 tons, but when all the competitors handled these comfortably, even in adverse wintry weather, this was increased to no less than 350 tons. It may have seemed that in staging these competitive trials the policy adopted was a complete negation of all Midland precepts. It must be emphasised, however, that the existing load limits were established to enable time to be kept by engines in the most run-down condition in which they could be accepted in traffic, whereas those selected for the trials were in first-class condition. The North Western people, indeed, complained that the particular compound, no. 1008, was too good,

21. St Pancras–Manchester express near Matlock, hauled by one of the 6 ft 9 in. compounds, no. 1047, built just after grouping.

having been recently out-shopped after general overhaul at Derby, whereas their own engine and the Midland 999 had both run a fair mileage in heavy traffic before the trials.

The compound certainly gave the best all-round results in the trials, with a much more splendid performance on a generally lower coal consumption than that of her rivals; but in the light of the subsequent record of engines of her class a heavily graded route favoured the performance characteristics of the design to an almost ideal extent. The results might not have been so favourable had the trials been conducted between Euston and Wolverhampton, where long sustained fast running was required. Even before the tests on the Leeds–Carlisle route had been completed authority had been given for construction of a further twenty Midland compounds differing only from the original design in having 6 ft 9 ins coupled wheels instead of 7 ft 0 in. They were numbered 1045 to 1064,

22. A McIntosh superheated 'Dunalastair IV' class 4–4–0, no. 14452 of the Caledonian, in red, leaving Aberdeen with a very heavy train in which the regular bogie corridor set has been reinforced by five flat-roofed, non-corridor eight-wheelers.

and six of them went new to Camden shed to take turns on the Euston–Birmingham–Wolverhampton expresses – much to the displeasure of ex-LNWR men. This batch of compounds had been completed at Derby by the early summer of 1924, and with the excellent results returned by engine no. 1008 in the first set of Leeds–Carlisle trials now apparent the decision was taken to build a further twenty, nos. 1065–84, with boiler mountings cut down so that they could work over the Scottish lines.

The Midland faction had by that time developed such a superiority-complex that they were prepared to challenge all comers, not merely the Class 4 engines of the constituent companies. A further series of Leeds–Carlisle trials were organised for the late autumn of 1924 in which new compounds of the 'short-chimneyed' series were to be set against an LNWR 4-cylinder 4–6–0 of the Claughton class. At the same time, in view of the impending use of the new compounds in Scotland, at Barr's request a Pickersgill 4–4–0 was included. As matters turned out those trials, run between 18 November and 10 December 1924 proved about the most unrepresentative of any in the history of the LMS. For the Midland side a standard 7 ft compound, sister engine of the brilliant 1008 of the earlier series of trials, had two days of dismally poor performance, losing time badly; and while two separate engines of the new short-chimneyed batch both did excellent work, it was at the expense of much higher coal consumption than no. 1008. The Caledonian 4–4–0, admittedly of no more than Class 3 capacity, could barely manage a 300-ton load, and that on a very heavy coal consumption, while the circumstances were so loaded against the Claughton and its crew as to produce another set of very inferior results. At that time Carlisle shed could not spare one for the trials, so instructions were given to Edge Hill to transfer one temporarily. Naturally in the absence of any other instructions the latter shed sent the worst they had!

The results were gratifying enough to justify the building of many more Midland compounds, and between May 1925 and July 1927 no fewer than 150 additional ones were added to the stock. But however the operating department might be yearning for a re-organisation of the entire LMS train service on Midland lines, it was clear to that of the Chief Mechanical Engineer that 3-cylinder compound 4–4–0s would not provide the ultimate answer to main line express train haulage requirements. In May 1925, only a few months before George Hughes retired, a carefully programmed series of dynamometer car trials was conducted between Carlisle and Preston, with LNWR and LYR 4–6–0s and a Midland compound. Therein was none of the rabid partisanship that had characterised earlier competitive trials. All four engines – Hughes 4–6–0, Prince of Wales, Claughton and compound – were in comparable condition; all four worked 350-ton trains, but in respect of their power classification the Prince and the compound (Class 4) also made runs with 300-ton trains, while the two Class 5 4-cylinder

4–6–0s ran with 400-ton trains. Again the, Midland compound, in this case no. 1065, proved best so far as the basic quantity of coal consumed per drawbar horsepower hour, but the margin of superiority was much narrower. Indeed, in running the 350-ton trains the Claughton had the lowest actual coal ·consumption of all. In any case the vaguely held notion that the LYR 4–6–0s were more economical than those of the LNWR was completely dispelled by these tests, which showed the complete opposite to be the case. At the time, however, and for some forty years subsequently no results of these tests were published.

When Hughes was succeeded as Chief Mechanical Engineer by Sir Henry Fowler, in 1925, and the headquarters of the department was transferred from Horwich to Derby, all thoughts for future development were in the way of compounds. There was first a 4–6–0 version of the ordinary Midland type, an engine which would have had the tractive power of the Royal Scots, of the future, but actually a much more handsome looking engine. In coming to Sir Henry Fowler's tenure of office as Chief Mechanical Engineer, however, one enters upon that period of LMS locomotive history when the balance of power and influence became delicately poised between the CME himself and the operating departments. At the same time Fowler himself was not pre-eminently a 'locomotive man', in the same sense as were Churchward, Bowen Cooke, and Gresley, to quote three of his contemporaries. His keen interests were in the back-room, as it were, in metallurgical problems particularly; and one gets the impression that he was not by any means 'sold' on compounds. On the other hand Anderson, who had to run the trains was convinced that the Midland compound was the best all-round engine for the job, and apparently sought no other.

23. An ex-LYR Hughes-type four-cylinder 4–6–0, no. 10465, leaving Oxenholme for Carlisle with a Liverpool and Manchester Scottish express.

F. R. Hebron, Rail Archive Stephenson

Then, while the Derby drawing office was feeling its way towards larger 3-cylinder compounds a paper read at the Graduates Section of the Institution of Mechanical Engineers early in 1926, by E. L. Diamond, had an influence that was quite astonishing for an occasion primarily intended for the more junior members of the profession. His subject was an investigation into the cylinder losses in a 3-cylinder compound locomotive. Not only was the meeting attended by Sir Henry Fowler himself, but subsequently Monsieur Bréville of the Northern Railway of France contributed some extremely important details of the working of his then-new 4-cylinder compound Pacifics. Fowler was so impressed that he set the Derby drawing office to work on the design of a huge compound Pacific for the West Coast main line of the LMS. In view of what eventually became the fate of a notable design another outcome of that paper at the Institution of Mechanical Engineers must be recalled.

Diamond's penetrating analysis into the cylinder performance of the Midland compounds, based upon the test results obtained with engine no. 1065 in the Leeds–Carlisle trials of 1924, showed how great was the loss due to

24. An unusually heavy down Midland express (ten coaches) climbing past Mill Hill, hauled by one of the later Midland compounds, no. 1097, in June 1926.

throttling both at admission and exhaust of steam from the cylinders at speeds of 65 to 70 mph and explained incidentally why the compounds were not at their best in high speed running. He recommended – daringly for a young man barely out of his pupilage! – that long-lap, long-travel valves should be generally adopted instead of the traditional valve gears then prevailing. Fowler was so impressed that he took the manuscript of the paper back to Derby with him, and told Herbert Chambers, his chief draughtsman, to scrap the valve gear

that was planned for a new series of 2–6–4 passenger tank engines, and design one in accordance with Diamond's recommendations. As a result the 2300 class, when it did appear, was one of the fastest, freest running, and most efficient locomotives the LMS ever had. It was, of course, a 2-cylinder simple – not a compound.

This incident is very important as showing that while Fowler was in no way an innovator so far as locomotive design was concerned he was quick enough to appreciate a good thing when he saw it, and this applied equally to the French 4-cylinder compound Pacifics. His own project in that direction had progressed sufficiently far

43

for him to obtain authority to build two engines of this design; and the frames had actually been cut before other events supervened. In the meantime the first steps had been taken towards an entirely new top-level organisation of the LMS, which was eventually to have a profound effect upon the locomotive department. As from 1 January 1926 the distinguished economist, Sir Josiah Stamp, had been appointed to the new office of President of the Executive; and although for the time being the veteran H. G. Burgess continued as General Manager, with Mathieson as deputy for Scotland, major changes were foreshadowed. In the locomotive department on the West Coast main line morale was at a low ebb, and with the imposition of Midland ideas, and with the infiltration of Midland compounds the old traditions of the LNWR seemed to have vanished. A single instance of express train running in April 1926,

from my own notebooks will provide a glimpse of an unhappy time.

6.23 pm PRESTON to EUSTON: Load: 374 tons tare, 400 tons full
Preston to Crewe: 4–4–0 no. 2577, 'Etna' (superheater Precursor)
Crewe to Rugby: Claughton no. 968, piloted by Midland compound no. 1151
Rugby to Euston: Claughton no. 98, piloted by Prince of Wales 4–6–0 no. 2198

The train was running fifteen minutes late, but the running was no more enterprising on the two sections south of Crewe, both double-headed, than on the section from Preston, where one 4–4–0 engine kept time. In earlier days no one would have dreamt of providing a pilot for a 374-ton load, and all drivers would have gone hard to make up time.

5
1926: A Critical and Decisive Year

The extent to which anti-Midland senti-
ments prevailed on the former LNWR
during the early years of grouping is exempli-
fied by the numbering of the locomotives concerned in my own journey referred to at the end
of the previous chapter; not a single engine had
been renumbered, and all of them still carried
the LNWR livery. To the four concerned south
of Preston could be added the Precursor that
worked our train from Barrow to Carnforth,
and the Prince of Wales 4–6–0 from Carnforth
to Preston. Then came the General Strike, on
4 May, which lasted for ten days. It was, of
course, very far from 'general' as far as the
railways were concerned, and on the LMS with
the aid of much volunteer labour, added to the
efforts of company's men who remained loyal
the service of passenger trains gradually increased until, on the last day, the LMS ran 1,865
trains. But after the end of the 'general' strike
the coal mines remained idle, and until alterna-
tive supplies of fuel could be organised it was
necessary to economise in the most drastic way
in the consumption of coal.

On the Western Division of the LMS not only
was the train service itself much reduced, but the
Midland-imposed engine loadings were aban-
doned and all double-heading vetoed. With the
restriction of train service the loads of individual
trains became very heavy, but the remarkable
thing was that in the emergency timetables the
scheduled times remained relatively fast. With
the 11.50 am, 2.35 pm and 2.55 pm departures
suspended, the 1.30 pm Scotsman out of Euston
carried some very heavy loads and yet was
allowed 94 minutes for the 82.6 miles to Rugby,
and 86 minutes for the continuing 75.5 miles to
Crewe. The ex-LNWR men seemed to delight
in showing what they could do in these difficult
conditions and I have details of timekeeping
runs with Claughtons no. 155, 'Sir Thomas
Williams', hauling 435 tons, no. 1429, 'Colonel
Lockwood', with 490 tons, and with an unnamed engine no. 162 with a full 500 tons. The
heaviest unpiloted load I personally observed
was one of 525 tons, on the one up day Scotch
express, which called additionally at Carnforth,
Lancaster, Preston, Wigan and Warrington,
and which was hauled unpiloted by another
Claughton no. 163, 'Holland Hibbert', still
finely turned out in the 'blackberry black'
livery. Moreover, with a load slightly reduced

25. Evidence of the coal shortage in 1926: one of the ex-LYR Hughes 4–6–0s, oil-fired, on a Bradford to Marylebone express at Huddersfield. Note the ex-GCR coach with Robinson anti-telescoping serrations just above the buffer beam.

to 485 tons, the train was taken forward from Crewe by a super-heated Precursor no. 1311, 'Napoleon', again in stout-hearted old style.

In view of such efforts it was ironical that, in the emergency service operated in the first few weeks after the end of the general strike, a drastically decelerated timetable was operated over the Midland Division. Against a normal schedule of 109 minutes non-stop over the 99.1 miles from St Pancras to Leicester no less than 128 minutes was allowed, an average speed of no more than 46.4 mph compared with the normal 54.5 mph and even then some trains were piloted! The situation that prevailed during the early summer of 1926 seemed to alert the operating authorities to the fact that they had in the Crewe express passenger locomotives units that were capable of far harder work than the Midland-imposed loading limits demanded, providing they were in good condition. In the continuing fuel emergency a break was made with the Derby operating philosophy by singling out those Claughtons that were in good condition, distinguishing them by a large letter 'S' on their cab sides, and increasing their maxi-

F. R. Hebron, Rail Archive Stephenson

26. An oil-fired Midland compound no. 1059, ready to leave St Pancras in June 1926, with a Kirtley 0–4–4 tank engine no. 1218 at right.

mum unpiloted load to 400 tons during the period of the summer service.

While the early years of grouping did not provide much inspiration in the way of new locomotive design, an interesting development in passenger coaching stock took place early in 1926 with the delivery from four British firms of a considerable number of steel carriages of a new design. These were notable as being of the open vestibule type, rather than having the traditional British compartments, and provided the first evidence of the influence of Mr R. W. Reid, the

Carriage and Wagon Superintendent of the LMS. While the bodies were of all-steel construction the interior finish was of polished mahogany in the majority of the new cars, although in some, experimentally, the interior finish was steel throughout. The cars had end doors only, and two windows per section of four seats on either side of the central gangway. It was significant of prevailing locomotive conditions that on the 'Invitation Run' of a set of these cars, from Euston to Birmingham, the train was hauled by a Claughton class engine still resplendent in the old LNWR livery!

An interesting development in traffic operating facilities on the Preston–Carlisle section of

27. An oil-fired 'Prince of Wales' class 4–6–0 no. 2198, 'John Ruskin', on a down LNWR express near Hatch End.

the West Coast main line was brought into service in 1926. Because of the greatly varying speeds of passenger and freight trains on this line, particularly on the heavy gradients north of Carnforth, facilities for shunting slower trains out of the path of faster ones had hitherto been provided by refuge sidings, the entry to which was made by shunting back over trailing points controlled by a signal box at the adjoining station. Such a movement was inevitably time consuming, but a direct access to such a refuge siding, by facing point connection would

usually have located such points beyond the limit for mechanical operation and required an additional signal-box. Developments in track circuiting and power signalling equipment made a neat solution of the problem available. At nine locations between Preston and Carlisle direct entry to running loops was provided by use of battery operated electric point machines controlled from existing signal boxes at the exit end of the loops. A local electricity supply was necessary at a time before the introduction of the National Grid. It was one of the first instances in Great Britain of remote controlled electric point layouts. The locations were Barton (down line);

28. An immaculate 'spinner', with tender piled high with 'ersatz' coal, ready to pilot a less elegant Class '3' Belpaire 4–4–0 on a London express at Nottingham.

Oubeck (down and up); Burton and Holme (down and up); Grayrigg (down and up); Tebay (down); Shap Summit, Thrimby Grange and Plumpton, all on up line; and Southwaite (down and up).

It was in 1923 that the celebrated Bridge Stress Committee had been set up by the Department of Scientific and Industrial Research, representing the Universities, the Ministry of Transport, the railways and the consulting engineers to Indian railways. One of its major tasks had been to establish a relation between the pulsating forces which were exerted by a locomotive when travelling at speed, and the consequent oscillation and stresses in the bridge. Although

its work was not published until 1929, by 1926 enough was known among the railway engineers concerned to enable some important decisions to be made as to locomotive utilisation on the LMS. The first concerned the Claughton class of the former LNWR. When Bowen Cooke put the design forward in 1911 it was rejected by the civil engineer, E. F. C. Trench, on account of the axle loading. He would not accept the argument that as there were four cylinders all driving on to the leading pair of coupled wheels the machinery was perfectly balanced and that there was no dynamic augment, or hammer blow, to add to the dead weight on the axles when running at high speed; and the original design had to be modified to the extent of using a smaller boiler.

49

29. One of the new steel-bodied coaches, with entrance doors only at the ends, introduced in 1926.

The work of the Bridge Stress Committee upheld Bowen Cooke's view, though some years after his death; and in view of the need for more powerful engines on the LNW section the Crewe drawing office worked out details of a larger boiler for the Claughtons. Whether reference was actually made to the original proposals of 1911 I cannot say. But this new proposition was enough to swell the mounting wave of opposition within the operating department towards the great 4-cylinder compound Pacific of Sir Henry Fowler, on which work had already started in the summer of 1926. The Claughtons had given such a good account of themselves in the fuel emergency following the general strike that an operating department inherently averse to very large engines began to feel that a modernised Claughton would be

good enough for their future needs, and they prevailed upon the top management to the extent that Sir Henry Fowler was instructed to stop work on his Pacific. Just exactly what happened in the higher councils of the LMS in the early autumn of 1926 has never been revealed; but it is known that Sir Guy Granet was on very friendly terms with Sir Felix Pole, of the Great Western, and it is more than likely that at some time he confided to him his misgivings about future locomotive power, and that the reply of Sir Felix would have been: 'Try one of ours.' As a result the 'Launceston Castle' was lent to the LMS. Before referring to the dynamometer car tests that were conducted, and their sequel, there is the momentous change in top level organisation on the LMS itself to be described.

From his taking up office as President of the

30. First of the Horwich Moguls (Crabs), no. 13000, introduced in 1926. The engine is here shown in photographic grey, though indicating the style of lining out adopted for the first livery in Midland red.

Executive in January 1926 Sir Josiah Stamp had been taking the measure of his new command and as from January 1927 four Vice-Presidents would take the place of the General Manager on an Executive Committee, which would be assisted by the Secretary and the Chief Legal Adviser. Announcement of the appointment of the four Vice-Presidents was made on 28 October 1926, as follows:

J. H. Follows: Railway Traffic Operating and Commercial Sections
S. H. Hunt: Railway Traffic Operating and Commercial
John Quirey: Accounting and service departments
R. W. Reid: Works and ancillary undertakings

Except for Hunt, who prior to the grouping had been Chief Goods Manager of the LNWR, all the new Vice-Presidents were ex-Midland men, and in his new appointment Reid, a former carriage and wagon man, became responsible for locomotives. With the retirement of D. A. Mathieson at the end of 1926 the direct influence of men of the pre-grouping Scottish companies became notably less.

The continuing absence of a settled policy of locomotive development was still evident in 1926, when a batch of twenty Pickersgill outside cylinder 4–6–0s of the 60 class were built. The six original engines of this design, first introduced in 1916, were distinguished more for their massive construction and relatively low maintenance costs than for their performance in traffic and general economy; but on Barr's recommendation these additional units were built, and one of them was put through a series of dynamometer car trials between Carlisle and Preston in the same conditions of working as observed by the four locomotives tested in May 1925 over the same route. The engine did better than I would have expected, though in no respect up to the quality of performance of the LNWR Prince of Wales class, also in the Class 4 category. The year 1926 also witnessed the final effort of the Lancashire and Yorkshire Railway as an independent locomotive activity in the production of the well-known Horwich 2–6–0 mixed traffic design. Aesthetically it was not a pretty engine, with the cylinders mounted high outside and quite steeply inclined. With the valve gear outside and readily accessible the action of the inclined 'works' gave rise to the nickname of 'Crabs', which lasted throughout their long and useful life.

As a postscript to the major organisational changes announced at the end of October 1926 three important new appointments were made to date from 1 January 1927, consequent upon the elevation of Messrs Follows, Hunt, and Reid to the office of Vice-Presidents:

C. R. Byrom: Chief General Superintendent

J. Ballantyne: Chief Goods Manager

E. J. H. Lemon: Carriage and Wagon Superintendent

These three new chief officers came from the LNWR, the Caledonian, and the Lancashire and Yorkshire respectively.

6
Drama of the 'Scots', and its Significance

This is not primarily a book about loco-motives, though any railway history is bound to be much concerned with the machines that move the traffic. But events in the last three months of 1926 on the LMS were of such significance, both to the *status quo* and to the whole future of the department that was the biggest spender on the railway, as to need a whole chapter for their recalling and close study. One must first look at some of the leading personalities involved. Sir Guy Granet, Chairman of the Company, was a mighty power in the land, and although he had come from the Midland experience of the first three years of grouping had convinced him that an entirely new approach to management was necessary, if his huge loosely-knit empire was not to continue as so many warring factions. It was not only from the Midland that there was top-class executive material. In finding a sol-ution to what could have been a delicate and frustrating matter of personnel Granet un-doubtedly looked back to his own entrée to the railway world. Unlike the great majority of his fellow general managers he had come in almost at the top. After taking a brilliant degree at Balliol College, Oxford, he was called to the

Bar in 1893, at the early age of twenty-six, and was appointed Secretary to the Railway Com-panies Association seven years later. In June 1905 he became Assistant General Manager of the Midland, and General Manager a year later. So likewise, in 1926, he installed Sir Josiah Stamp, as President of the Executive of the LMS.

To appreciate the drastic action taken over the head of the Chief Mechanical Engineer in 1926 the enterprising plans for train service develop-ment for the following summer must be re-called. Ideas for re-casting the service on the LNW section on Midland lines had receded, and with C. R. Byrom, an ex-North Western man designated as the new Chief General Superin-tendent the development was definitely being planned on traditional West Coast lines, with heavier loads than could be handled by the 'S' designated Claughtons. The great Pacifics that Sir Henry Fowler was engaged upon would obviously take some time to develop from the prototypes into effective traffic machines, and could not be expected to take any appreciable part in the improved summer services planned for 1927. In recording the stoppage of work on the Pacifics in the *Railway Magazine* of

F. R. Hebron, Rail Archive Stephenson

31. All Western Division trains light enough to be hauled by Midland compounds? The first portion of the 10 am Scottish express from Euston in August 1926, at Bushey troughs hauled by no. 1159. The second part that followed was hauled by no. 1124.

November 1926, the late Cecil J. Allen, as usual very well informed as to internal happenings on the LMS, added that recourse would probably be made to more Claughtons, with larger boilers. To have written thus he would need to have had the information not later than mid-September.

The high management of the LMS, going clean above the head of their Chief Mechanical Engineer, then made arrangements to borrow a Great Western Castle class 4–6–0, and instructions were given to the operating department,

and to Sir Henry Fowler to put it through a series of dynamometer car trials between Euston and Carlisle. Because of structural restrictions it could not be run north of the Border. A note in the December 1926 issue of the *Railway Magazine* stated that the Castle had been running against a Claughton, no. 1093, 'Sir Guy Calthrop'; but there was actually no competitive running. At about the same time the Claughton in question had been running dynamometer car trials between Crewe and Carlisle in another connection altogether, and this may have led to some jumping to wrong conclusions. As might be expected the Castle put up an impressive performance, though north of Crewe it did not equal, let alone surpass the

F. R. Hebron, Rail Archive Stephenson

32. The train that was introduced before the new engines were ready. The up 'Royal Scot' in 1927, non-stop Carnforth to Euston, passing Tring hauled by 4–4–0 no. 5384, 'S. R. Graves', and 'Claughton' no. 5958.

finest work that had been done by Claughtons in the past. For one thing the dry sanding gear of the Great Western engine did not prove very effective in the bad weather conditions encountered between Carnforth and Carlisle. But the demonstration was enough to convince the operating department that a 4–6–0 with a nominal tractive effort of around 32,000 lb, would fulfil all their requirements. There was no need to go to a Pacific such as that on which work was already started.

So far as time was concerned, however, the situation was rapidly becoming desperate. The last of the dynamometer car trials was not completed until 20 November, and at once Fowler was instructed to get fifty engines of comparable power to the Castle built and ready for the summer service of 1927 – *fifty!* None of the railway workshops was in a position to build engines of such size and power in the time, even if drawings were immediately available. The CME's department was indeed in a very tight corner. It was a humiliating position for Fowler himself, and a man of less equable personality could well have deepened the crisis by resigning forthwith. The job would have to be put out to contract, though at the end of November no one, even in the Derby drawing office, knew what the engines were to be like. Desperate

55

33. The first of the new engines, no. 6100, 'Royal Scot' at Crewe.

measures were tried. First of all the Great Western was asked to build fifty Castles – more than they had ever previously (or since) built for themselves in one year, let alone six months. When this was refused Derby asked for a set of drawings; this also was refused, and then, continuing the humiliating process, an appeal was made to R. E. L. Maunsell, whose brand new 'Lord Nelson' was another near equivalent to what the operating department had stipulated. The Southern were, of course, delighted to know that their help had been sought in such a dilemma, and after Herbert Chambers had been to Waterloo and laid his difficulties before J. Clayton and H. Holcroft, a complete set of working drawings was sent to Glasgow, to the North British Locomotive Company.

Up at Hyde Park the drawing office must have worked like lightning, because on 7 December 1926, less than a month after the end of

the Castle trials, they submitted their quotation. The work was to be divided between the Hyde Park and the Queens Park Works, twenty-five engines to each; delivery was to commence twenty-five weeks after acceptance of the quotation and to be completed in thirty-five weeks. The quotation was accepted on 23 December 1926, but because of the holidays at Christmas and the New Year the orders were not placed at the two works until 7 January 1927. Even with the vast experience of the North British Locomotive Company available it was a tremendous project. The drawings of the 'Lord Nelson' would undoubtedly have been of some assistance, but Derby could contribute little from past experience towards the design of a locomotive so very much larger than anything that had gone before. Certain Midland specialities, like brakes on the bogie wheels, and the Fowler-and-Anderson by-pass valves on the cylinders were specified; but the basic design was worked out in the NBL drawing office, with the

34. Light work for one of the Polmadie-based 'Scots':
no. 6128, later named 'Meteor', climbing to Beattock
summit with a seven-coach southbound express.

friendly, guiding hand of Herbert Chambers
always available. It is amusing to recall that in
contemporary LMS internal correspondence the
new engines were referred to as 'Improved
Castles'! The 'improvement' presumably, was
to use three cylinders instead of four.

The design of the boiler and firebox of the
new LMS 4–6–0 showed clearly the influence of
the 'Lord Nelson'. The diameters of the small
tubes, superheater flues, and superheater elements were the same, and the shapes of the fire-
boxes were practically identical. But while the
'Nelson' had the Maunsell superheater the LMS
engine had the Derby version of the Schmidt.
Midland influence was apparent also in the
adoption of a chimney with a parallel bore – a
most unlikely design to provide the necessary
draught for free steaming. The 'Lord Nelson'

had the more usual tapered interior, shaped to
conform with the divergent cone of exhaust
steam from the blast pipe. Theory apart, however, and in flat contradiction to what one might
have expected, the Royal Scots, as the new LMS
4–6–0s became, proved far more reliable
steamers in heavy working than the 'Nelsons'.
Although the cylinders were designed in
accordance with the principles adopted for the
2–6–4 tanks of the 2300 class, with long-lap,
long-travel valves, the piston valves were of the
traditional Schmidt type with a single, wide
ring, as had been standard on the Midland for
many years. Another Midland feature, applied
to a most vital component, was the use of
manganese bronze driving axle boxes.

Seeing that the engine was designed in such a
shipwreck hurry the result was remarkably successful, though Sir Henry Fowler himself can
have contributed little. The experience of the

35. Aftermath of an engine failure: a 'Precedent' class 2–4–0, no. 5069, 'Penrith Beacon' has to tackle a load estimated at 420 tons, unaided, past Hest Bank in 1927.

North British Locomotive Company in producing large engines for arduous service was invaluable in securing a machine that was structurally robust, and the boilermaking was superb. The weaknesses, some of which took time to reveal themselves, lay in the incorporation of features of design that were adequate enough for the lightly-loaded and gently treated Midland 4–4–0 engines, but which did not stand up to the heavy service involved in working the principal West Coast expresses. While the design as a whole could be regarded as a hotch-

potch of different ideas, it eventually proved a very successful one. A glaring example of hasty improvisation was to be seen in the tender. There was little enough time to design the engine itself, let alone a new tender; and one cannot blame Chambers for taking the standard Midland 3,500-gallon type, and attaching it to the 'Scot'. The fact that it was considerably narrower than the cab of the new engine was incidental – until one rode in the seat on the fireman's side and looked back into an airy nothing!

Despite Herculean efforts in Glasgow, at both main works, the NBL did not quite maintain the exiguous delivery dates required by the contract

36. One of the new Moguls, no. 13065, in red, leaving Nottingham with an excursion train.

and the first engine did not arrive at Derby until 14 July, nearly a fortnight late, and the next ones were not ready until three weeks later. In any case they could not have been available for the inauguration of the new Royal Scot train service on 11 July 1927. Then, the unprecedented step was taken of making the time-honoured 10 am West Coast expresses in each direction exclusive to London–Glasgow and London–Edinburgh passengers, with division of the train at Syming-ton. With no more than existing locomotive power available a stop to change engines was made at Carnforth, with ex-LNW power south of that point, and a pair of Scottish-allocated Midland compounds on the northern section of the journey. The minimum load was to be fifteen of the latest LMS coaches, or about 420 tons tare, and in the prevailing conditions with 'S' designated Claughtons this involved double heading throughout. Of course, with such a relatively generous allowance as 265 minutes for the 236 miles between Euston and Carnforth, an average speed of no more than 53.4 mph, Claughtons in their best form would have had no difficulty in taking the fifteen-coach train without assistance; but in 1927 the circum-stances were not those of 1913–16! On the Royal

Scot train of 1927 the pilots were always 4–4–0s of the George the Fifth class.

The first of the Royal Scot locomotives no. 6100, arrived in the south of England nameless, and its massive proportions were first revealed to the railway enthusiast fraternity in a splendid photograph taken in Euston station, and reproduced as frontispiece to the *Railway Magazine* of September 1927. I think we were all a bit staggered by the diameter of the boiler; but looking at that picture today one can appreciate what a really elegant engine the original Royal Scot was. By September sufficient of the fifty had been delivered to enable the operating department to change the working of the Royal Scot trains to what they had originally planned; to a non-stop run between Euston and Carlisle, with one of the new engines, and division of the train as previously at Symington. At the time I think there can have been few of us who fully appreciated just what that Euston–Carlisle non-stop run was going to mean as an all-weather task during the winter months. True, the booked average speeds were not very high: 52 mph going north, and 50.5 mph southbound. But the men were at work for nearly six hours, non-stop, and those standard Midland tenders carried no more than $5\frac{1}{2}$ tons of coal. Even allowing for the careful high-stacking of coal on the tenders, and what was in the firebox at the start, it did not allow for a consumption of more than about 50 lb per mile. While every consideration had been given to making the new engines very economical, there would be times when adverse weather, or other circumstances would force the coal consumption up, willy-nilly, if the enginemen were to keep their schedule times.

It was a heroic gesture, in the way of train running, and it succeeded beyond belief. The Euston–Carlisle 'non-stops' brought some splendid and long overdue publicity to the affairs of the LMS, and the reliability with which those long runs were made during the winter of 1927–8 was a remarkable tribute to the design and construction work that had been put into the locomotives. Another factor not perhaps generally realised was that *all* the enginemen so involved had to 'learn the road' over considerable mileages. The work was shared between Camden and Carlisle sheds. The former, and only a few men at that, had not previously worked north of Carnforth, while the Carlisle men had not previously worked south of Crewe. The top link men at Crewe North shed, who did know the road throughout from Euston to Carlisle, were busy road learning northwards from Carlisle to Glasgow, and later to Perth, for new double-home turns with the new engines.

7

The Emergent New Railway

Quite apart from the spectacular non-stop running of the Royal Scot between Euston and Carlisle, the latter half of the year 1927 showed unmistakable evidence of the new philosophy of management that was being developed on the LMS. Under the influence of Sir Josiah Stamp, there was a growing encouragement to the staff to 'think LMS', rather than in terms of one or other of the constituent companies. There were beginnings of a co-ordination in facilities that had previously been duplicated by the activities of the pre-grouping railways, and an awareness that the whole organisation had got to be geared to more modern conditions, and the increasingly severe competition of road transport. The naming of many of the principal express trains, not only on the North Western but also on the Midland routes, was evidence of the publicity drive that was beginning. In this the famous West Coast 'Corridor' – the afternoon Anglo-Scottish service – became the Midday Scot, and the Irish Mail, one of the oldest named trains in the world, at last carried its name on the carriage roof boards.

One former North Western train to be distinguished by a name, the 'Ulster Express', was the Fleetwood–Belfast boat express, truly one of the really 'crack' locomotive workings of the old LNWR; but it did not last long in its old form. From 30 April 1928 the service was transferred to the former Midland packet station at Heysham Harbour, to which there also ran a boat train from St Pancras, at 5 pm. This, of course, was not a serious competitor to the 6.10 pm from Euston for London traffic, but it gathered Irish business from its various intermediate stops on the Midland line. But the switch in the case of the North Western train from Fleetwood to Heysham meant there was only one LMS steamer instead of two sailing nightly to Belfast. This was fed by a third train that originated at Leeds Central at 7.15 pm and travelled over the Lancashire and Yorkshire line via Manchester, calling at Low Moor, Halifax, Sowerby Bridge, Todmorden, and Rochdale. West of Manchester it called at Bolton and Chorley, running non-stop from the last mentioned station to Lancaster. I travelled by it several times, but it was not a very exciting train from the speed point of view.

The transfer of 'The Ulster Express' from Fleetwood to Heysham was marked by the introduction of three fine new steamers, the

37. Aberdeen–Glasgow Pullman car express passing Luncarty. Although the engines, McIntosh 4–4–0 no. 14458 and Pickersgill 4–4–0 no. 14505, are both resplendent in Midland red, the train includes many vehicles still in the old colours.

'Duke of Lancaster', 'Duke of Argyll' and the 'Duke of Rothesay'. While it was not correct, as the *Railway Magazine* did at the time, to claim them as the fastest ships on any cross-Channel service, because the mail steamers on the Holyhead–Dun Laoghaire run held this distinction, by a considerable margin, they were certainly the most luxuriously equipped. They were modelled on the general principles of ocean liners. Sleeping accommodation was provided for 308 saloon, and 104 steerage passengers, the former class including four cabines-de-luxe, 141 single berth rooms, 65 double-berth cabins and seven four-berth rooms. The ships, which were built by William Denny Bros, of Dumbarton, were of 3,600 tons, and capable of a speed of 21 knots. The three connecting trains arrived at 10.50 pm from the LYR line, 11 pm from St Pancras, via Sheffield, and Leeds, and 11.1 – optimistic scheduling here! – from Euston. The steamer left at 11.50 pm and was due at Belfast (Donegal Quay) at 6.30 am. It gave opportunity for a good night's rest – the Irish Sea being willing – and time for a leisurely breakfast before a day's business. On the eastbound run one could board the ship in the early evening and enjoy dinner before the departure at 9.40 pm. Next morning

38. One of the 25-knot Irish Mail steamers on the Holyhead–Dunlaoghaire run, the *Cambria*, at Holyhead.

the connecting trains left Heysham at 6.10 am for Manchester and the LYR line, 7 am for Euston, and 7.16 for Leeds and Midland stations. This latter ran combined with the Morecambe–Bradford 'club' train, which was divided from it at Skipton.

Among the named trains introduced in 1927 were three on the Midland Division. The morning Scotch Expresses between St Pancras, Edinburgh and Glasgow became the 'Thames–Forth', and 'Thames–Clyde' expresses respectively, and the direct St Pancras–Bradford trains, running via Thornhill (by-passing Leeds) be-

came the 'Yorkshireman': 9.10 am up from Bradford Exchange, and 4.55 pm down from St Pancras. On the North Western section I must tell of an amusing incident concerning the morning and evening service between Manchester and Euston, at first named the 'Mancunian'. I was travelling by the 3.20 pm down from Marylebone one afternoon (Great Central route) and heard a fellow-traveller explaining to his companion with considerable *impressement*, that this very important train was called the 'Manchurian', presumably running via the Harwich–Zeebrugge train ferry, Berlin, Moscow, and the Trans-Siberian Railway!

39. Resignalling at Manchester: the approach lines to Victoria from Miles Platting. The inward bound signals were four-aspect colour lights, while the outward signals from the station remained as semaphores.

An important piece of traffic working rationalisation, with which as a young engineer I had some connection, was the linking up of certain facilities at the adjoining Victoria and Exchange stations in Manchester, formerly L&Y, and LNW owned. The work involved complete resignalling at the western end of the area, and was interesting as the first installation of day colour light signals anywhere on the LMS system. Both the London and North Western and the Lancashire and Yorkshire Railways had been extensive users of power signalling, but hitherto with traditional lower-quadrant semaphore signals. At Manchester the newly established code of four-indication colour light signals was adopted, using the short-lived 'cluster' type of signal head, in cases of awkward sighting. At that time in LMS history the signal superintendents were assistant engineers in the department of the Chief Civil Engineer, and the designer of the Manchester installation was R. G. Berry, a former LYR man, and a delightful personality. His colleague on the electrical side was H. W. Moore.

There were times when, as contractors, we needed all the goodwill they could muster, because some of their civil engineering overlords were not always so flexible in their attitudes. It was one of my tasks to work out the operating connections for the electric point machines, and to devise an arrangement that would suit LNW and L&Y, as well as the new British standard switches, which existed in about equal numbers in the area concerned. In this, we, contractors and railway signal engineers alike, soon came into head-on collision with the new Chief Civil Engineer of the LMS.

64

40. One of the huge Beyer-Garratt 2–6–0+0–6–2
locomotives on a train of coal empties near Hendon on
14 July 1928.

H. C. Casserley

E. F. C. Trench, formerly of the LNWR, had recently retired from this high office, and had been succeeded by Alexander Newlands, from the Highland. I mention the following incident to show how different was his attitude, in a difficulty, from that of Sir Henry Fowler. The question came up of fitting to the switch blades the extension pieces to which the rods for operating the electric detector contacts in the point machine had to be attached. The usual practice at the time was to drill additional holes in the switch blades, but Newlands would have none of it, and when one of our engineers, thinking to be helpful, produced a drawing showing what we were currently doing on the Southern, for the big installation then in hand for London Bridge he retorted, with positively withering scorn: 'Don't you think we are a large enough organisation to decide for ourselves, without considering what the Southern Railway are doing!'

On the former Lancashire and Yorkshire Railway H. W. Moore and R. G. Berry had together developed a distinctive form of route indicator for displaying the platform into which a train was to be routed at a large terminal station. It had been used in conjunction with pneumatically operated semaphore signals at Southport, not long before the grouping; but at Manchester an entirely optical projector type of route indicator was used. It had been developed by Westinghouse, primarily for use on the Southern and consisted of a nest of projector units, each containing a stencilled figure or letter. The particular indication to be displayed

41. Down express goods train on Dillicar troughs, hauled by a Whale 19-inch 4–6–0. With such a load as that seen here, the train would probably have stopped at Tebay for rear-end banking assistance to Shap summit.

was selected electrically and projected onto a ground glass screen. It was ingenious in conception, but in the smoky atmosphere that prevailed around large towns the screen soon became coated with soot, and the illuminated indication barely visible. One could not clean it, because the ground surface of the glass had to be outwards to give clear definition, and the application of a rag, with any grease on it would be fatal to the surface. That type of route indicator did not last long in Great Britain, though I saw some that had been installed about the same time

in the clean air of Bombay still in service fifty years later!

The Midland tradition of having naught but moderate powered locomotives was adequate enough for the passenger service operated up to the time of grouping, though the rigid limitations of loading involved a good deal of piloting at times of holiday traffic, as was always to be remembered from the circumstances leading up to the tragic disaster north of Hawes Junction in the early hours of Christmas Eve, 1910. But so far as the regular, very heavy mineral traffic of the company was concerned it was a complete anachronism. Every day train after train of coal toiled its way southwards

42. Down 'Lakes' express passing Oxenholme hauled by four-cylinder 4–6–0 no. 5916, 'E. Tootal Broadhurst', 'Claughton' class.

from Toton Yard to Cricklewood invariably double-headed. The Beyer-Garratt type of articulated locomotive was an admirable, though by Midland traditions a sensational answer to this uneconomic way of working. The great engines introduced in 1927 were the equivalent, in tractive effort, of a Class 3 and a Class 4 0–6–0 combined, 45,620 lbs. With a grate area of 44.5 sq. ft, the original engines of the type had conventional coal bunkers carrying 7 tons of coal, but the later ones had the revolving self-trimming type with a capacity of 9 tons, which made things easier for the fire-men. I have always understood that too many Derby specialities were specified for the liking of Beyer, Peacock & Co., who always liked a fairly free hand in designing Garratts. In any case, they came quite early in the Beyer-Garratt saga, and were not to be compared in perfection of design with some of the later, and quite outstanding products of the firm. Nevertheless, they were a tremendous forward step on a route where only small engines, in multiple, had previously been used.

So far as express passenger motive power was concerned, having got the fifty Royal Scots into service Crewe Works was given the go-ahead for the enlarged Claughtons, though this took the form of rebuilding some of the existing engines rather than building new ones. Altogether twenty engines of the class were so treated, ten retaining their original cylinders and motion, and ten fitted with the Caprotti valve gear. This followed extended trials of that gear on one of the original Claughtons, no. 5908, 'Alfred Fletcher'. This was one of the ten to receive larger boilers and the Caprotti gear. The nominal tractive effort was increased in proportion to the increased boiler pressure from 175 to 200 lbs per sq. in. The rebuilt engines were designated Class 5X, as being mid-way between the Class 5 of the original Claughtons, and the Class 6 of the Royal Scots. They were distributed between Preston, Longsight, and Holyhead sheds, those at the latter taking over the entire working of the Irish Mails. For some time prior to this a batch of original Claughtons had been working the Irish Mails through over the 263 miles between Euston and Holyhead, with the men working on a double-home basis. It was the longest through working undertaken by the original Claughtons, and published data shows that they made a good job of it.

One of the records in respect of long through workings of LMS locomotives up to that time – non-stop into the bargain – came on Friday 27 April 1928. On the following Tuesday, 1 May, the LNER were to inaugurate the world's record daily non-stop run with 'The Flying Scotsman', over the $392\frac{3}{4}$ miles between Kings Cross and Edinburgh. It was to be a remarkable achievement, made possible by carrying two engine crews, with one relieving the other at the half-way point via the corridor tender devised by H. N. Gresley. But without any previous announcement the LMS decided to break the new record before it had been made. Arrangements were made to run the Glasgow and Edinburgh portions of the Royal Scot separately, and for both to run non-stop from London to the Scottish cities: 399.7 miles from Euston to Edinburgh and 401.4 miles from Euston to Glasgow. Both runs were punctually made. The nine-coach Glasgow portion was hauled by a Royal Scot, no. 6113, 'Cameronian', and the Edinburgh section of six coaches by a Midland compound, no. 1054. At that time LMS regulations did not allow more than three men on an engine in ordinary traffic, and for this special occasion a call for volunteers was made. The crews consisted of two drivers one each from the Western and the Scottish Divisions, and one fireman, it being understood that the drivers would take some share in the firing when not actually at the regulator. Both sections of the train were successfully worked comfortably within the $6\frac{1}{4}$-hour schedule then operating between London and the Scottish Cities.

8
Locomotives: Performance, Economics, Maintenance

After the blaze of publicity that accompanied the introduction of the Royal Scots in 1927, and the technical details of dynamometer car test runs with engine no. 6100 given by Sir Henry Fowler himself at a meeting of the Institution of Mechanical Engineers on 16 December 1927, a great and ultimately significant silence fell over the LMS locomotive scene. The figures of basic coal consumption that he quoted, varying between 2.66 and 3.33 lb per drawbar horsepower hour were. an astonishing improvement upon the general level of 4 to 5 lb returned by older locomotives in the dynamometer car trials conducted in 1924–5. There were some people, including Gresley of the LNER, who did not believe them; and on the pretext that he thought his own dynamometer car (that of the former North Eastern Railway) was out of adjustment, it was arranged for it to be tested against the Horwich car used in the Royal Scot trials. The result was amusing in that *both* cars were found to be wrong!

Performance on the Euston–Carlisle non-stop runs of the Royal Scot train was good. The small links of enginemen at Camden and Carlisle sheds had been specially selected, and

briefed, but elsewhere the new locomotives were allocated to the sheds and put into traffic without any particular instructions. The original distribution of the 50 locomotives was Camden, 16; Rugby 3; Crewe North 9; Edge Hill 9; Carlisle 7; and Polmadie 6. Some of the ex-North Western men tried to handle them as they would have done a George the Fifth or a Prince of Wales, and were disappointed to find that the engines apparently had no 'go' in them. With loads not exceeding about 400 tons many of the men definitely preferred a Claughton; and then, before they had generally 'got the hang' of working them the class as a whole began to show an alarming increase in coal consumption. In the ordinary way this might have been acknowledged as just one of those things that occur with all locomotives as running mileage mounts up, if – and it was a very crucial 'if' – the working diagrams had been the same as in LNWR days, with a maximum length of continuous through running of just under 200 miles, Euston to Liverpool.

With the Scots, however, in addition to the 299-mile Euston–Carlisle turns, both Crewe-North and Polmadie sheds had 243-mile runs between Crewe and Glasgow, while there was

43. The Beyer-Ljungstrom turbo-condensing locomotive, built in 1927, on trial on the Midland line.

at least one 290-mile turn between Crewe and Perth. With those small tenders and coal consumption rising to more than 50 lb per mile, there was constant risk of running out of coal. On several runs that I logged personally on the Crewe–Glasgow workings there was every sign that the drivers were doing what they could to conserve coal – going easily uphill, often dropping a minute or so on their booked point to point times – and then running fast downhill to recover what time they could. On the timings then in operation the load for a Scot between Euston and Carnforth was 500 tons, but with tare loads of more than 450 tons, the north-

bound Royal Scot train usually stopped for a pilot at Oxenholme.

The cause of this rapid deterioration might have remained a matter for conjecture had not Sir Josiah Stamp not instituted a system of individual costing of locomotives. The bill for locomotive maintenance and repair was a big one, and as a master statistician he wanted to know where the money was going, not merely in a general way but what was spent on *every single locomotive*. At first there were some in the department who felt this was bureaucracy run mad, but before long it was appreciated as a magnificent tool of management. The rapid rise in coal consumption of the Royal Scots was immediately revealed, and the most urgent steps

44. The super-high-pressure compound 4–6–0 no. 6399, 'Fury', as built in 1929.

were taken to ascertain its cause. From being the pride and joy of the line these fifty big engines had soon become dangerously suspect. In some cases the increase was nearly 80 per cent above their consumption per train mile when they were new. When this meant they were using some 70 lb per mile it was no wonder that drivers were getting anxious on the long runs.

After some careful experimenting it was found that the trouble lay in the single wide rings of the Schmidt type piston valves. It was an insidious form of failure, because when wear developed on these rings they permitted a considerable amount of internal leakage of steam. It was not an obvious leak, like a blowing gland, and it was one that had little significance on lightly worked engines like the Midland 4–4–0s, on which the Schmidt type ring had been standard on superheater engines. On heavily worked engines like the Royal Scots it became serious. The answer was found in using solid valve heads, with six narrow rings. It worked like a charm, and brought coal consumption down, on the same duties, from 70 to 35 lb per mile! It was so successful that it was also applied to the Claughtons, and resulted in an equally gratifying reduction in coal consumption. Some dynamometer car test runs made with the latter engines, over the Leeds–Carlisle road, in another connection, showed that the basic coal

Author's collection

71

45. Mr H. P. M. Beames, formerly Chief Mechanical Engineer of the LNWR, and later principal architect of the very successful works reorganisation at Crewe.

consumption had been brought down from the 4½ lb of coal per drawbar horsepower hour of the engines in their LNWR condition to 3½ lb with the new solid-head piston valves and six narrow rings.

In the *Railway Magazine* for April 1913 there had appeared a lengthy article under the title 'The most famous railway works in the world: Crewe–London and North Western Railway'. A few weeks later the works was honoured by a visit from King George V and Queen Mary, the first occasion ever when a railway works was

visited by the reigning sovereign and his consort. The tremendous strain subsequently put upon its manufacturing facilities during the First World War had left it in urgent need of re-organisation. The first thoughts towards this were given while C. J. Bowen Cooke was still alive; but his untimely death, the amalgamation with the Lancashire and Yorkshire Railway, then the grouping postponed the inauguration of the plan, and it was not until March 1925, under the immediate direction of H. P. M. Beames, that the work of re-organisation began. The underlying feature of the scheme was the introduction into the erecting and repairing shops of the processing or 'Belt'

72

F. R. Hebron, Rail Archive Stephenson

46. The 'Claughtons' still on first-class duties: engine no. 5936, unnamed, passing Tring with a down Manchester express.

system, which at that time had been more closely associated with mass-production in the automobile industry. Quite apart from the 'Old Works' in the vee between the main and Chester lines at Crewe North Junction, the works had grown up piecemeal over the years until, in 1918, there were no fewer than 256 engine pits, extending over *nine* erecting shops, and the time spent over a heavy overhaul occupied anything between thirty and fifty days.

The 'Belt' system installed in the re-organised works ensured that the locomotives in the erecting shop and the components in the various stages passed forward from stage to stage in the correct sequence. The underlying principles were:

(a) that work should be moved to the men, rather than men to work

47. A strange locomotive combination: a train for East Anglia leaving Nottingham hauled by a yellow-painted M&GN engine, but piloted by an ex-Midland 0–6–4 tank no. 2000, of the class nicknamed the 'flat irons'.

(b) that work should be carried out continuously – that is, that any task undertaken should be pushed through to completion without any intermediate delays.

It is remarkable that with the total number of engine pits reduced from 256 to no more than 72, the time of heavy overhaul for the largest engines – which at the time of completion of the reorganisation scheme were the 4-cylinder Claughton class 4–6–0s – had been reduced to a maximum of twelve days. The greatly reduced time of overhaul, of course, meant that fewer

locomotives were needed to work the traffic. It is important to appreciate that the scheme of re-organisation was completed in 1927, before any save ex-LNWR locomotives were being maintained at the works.

The new erecting shop, at the extreme west end of the works area, had three bays, each with two pit roads, or belts. The complete shop provided on the six belts seventy-two repair stages in all. Of the twelve stages for each engine the first two were devoted to stripping; an engine, when this work was completed, going forward to one of the succeeding four stages, during which time repairs were carried out on the frames, cylinders and so on. The work gangs, of which there were four, moved between stages 1, 2, 3 and 4 as they finished their

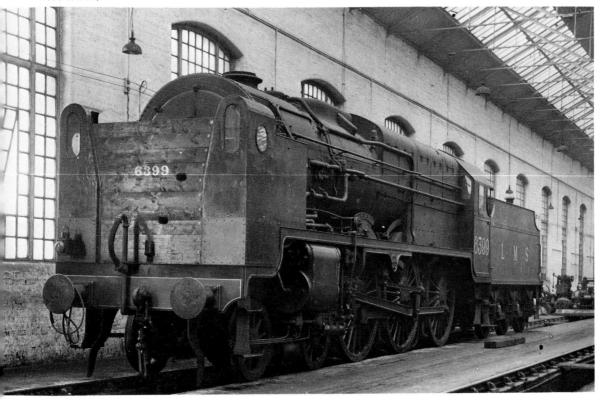

48. 'Fury' after the disastrous blow-back at Carstairs on 18 September 1932, still with indicator shelters fitted, back in Derby works.

own particular tasks. Only four working days were allowed for an engine to remain on its stand, and on the fifth day the engine was lowered on its bogie and intermediate wheels. It was a magnificent piece of workshop organisation. The first locomotive to be repaired by this system was turned out on 5 May 1927, and since that time the sustained output had been sixteen repaired locomotives a week. These it should be emphasised were complete general overhauls with every engine concerned stripped down to its frames. The standardisation of detail parts, and the relatively few major locomotive classes on the former LNWR naturally helped in achieving such results. At the time of the inauguration of the system only ex-LNWR classes were involved. Although, by May 1927, there were a number of ex-LYR 4–6–0s and Midland compounds and Class 4F 0–6–0s working on the Western Division, the former went to Horwich for general repairs and the latter two classes to Derby.

It must of course be appreciated that while by far the largest part of the re-organisation concerned the repair of locomotives, new construction was at all times proceeding apace, though no longer with locomotives of North Western design. New construction included 2–6–0 mixed traffic engines of the Horwich type, which when first put into traffic were painted Midland red, and standard Class 4F 0–6–0s of the Midland type. Work at Crewe in 1928 also included the rebuilding of twenty Claughtons with the large boiler. By that time also repainting of the locomotives was at last fully in hand, though quite apart from the colour which was still distasteful to North Western eyes, the Midland practice of pairing engines with specific tenders, essential by the carrying of the engine number in huge figures on the tender, did not suit Crewe. The North Western put any tender with any engine, and in the early days of the red livery some odd things happened. Not only did the numbers on engine and tender disagree, but the classes got mixed, and one saw, for example, a Prince of Wales 4–6–0 with a tender numbered in the George the Fifth series, or worse still, a red engine with a black tender, and vice versa.

Even the Midland Division did not escape from this kind of mix-up, as the prelude to one of the finest runs I ever had between Carlisle and Leeds showed. I was travelling on the 12 noon from Edinburgh (Waverley) to St Pancras, and after the North British Atlantic had coupled off

at Carlisle the fresh engine came backing down with '1108' in the usual huge figures on her tender. I was about to enter the number in my log book when I spotted a small '1070' inside the cab; and going forward to confirm I saw indeed that we had compound no. 1070, with 1108's tender! This was certainly unusual on the Midland. Although it is briefly carrying the locomotive story a few years forward I must add that Derby locomotive works was also subjected to extensive reorganisation, though not to the extent of installing the 'Belt' system of progression through the erecting shops. Even so, a high output of approximately twenty general repairs a week was secured. It is interesting to recall that at the time this reorganisation was put into operation both the Works Superintendent, H. G. Ivatt, and the Assistant Works Superintendent, R. A. Riddles, were ex-Crewe men, both of whom, as is well known, rising in after years to positions of great eminence in the locomotive world.

9
Scotland: 1927–1930

In the early autumn of 1927 I travelled north of Perth for the first time, and for the next three years all my annual leave was spent somewhere in the Highlands. Added to these visits were a number of Bank Holiday week-end trips to the English Lakes, or the Border country, on which I always contrived to include Carlisle in my itineraries. So, although my favours both for sightseeing and railway interests had to be divided between the LMS and the LNER, I did see a good deal of the LMS in those uncertain, barely formative years, before my professional work took me to Scotland for longer stays. In the first years covered by this chapter, apart from engine and carriage colours, there was really less evidence of grouping on the LMS than on the LNER. There were Midland compounds stationed at both Kingmoor and Polmadie, and units from the former shed had three double-home turns to Aberdeen. Thence they worked south on the early morning London express, the up Postal, and the 'Royal Highlander'. The last mentioned, with a heavy sleeping car section, was regularly double-headed. Apart from this mild incursion, the whole line from Glasgow and Edinburgh northward to Wick, Thurso and Kyle of Lochalsh was solidly pre-grouping in its locomotive power.

The new English overlords, first at Horwich and then at Derby, seemed to form a very high opinion of the Highland engines. Certainly they were a massively built, trouble-free lot, and all were agreed that they looked well in Midland red. Although it had been well maintained one had to admit that the dark unlined green of the final Highland days was not the most attractive of engine liveries. I saw a few of them still in the old colours, and they looked somewhat drab. The second batch of Clan class 4–6–0s, added in 1922, in light green, were much more pleasing to the eye. But for doing the work the Highland engines as a whole were, within their several ranges of tractive power, among the finest ever. Both Castles and Clans had boilers that would steam freely under the most severe and continuous pounding, and both fully justified their LMS power classifications of 3 and 4. The last Locomotive Superintendent of the Highland Railway had been David Urie, a son of the Chief Mechanical Engineer of the London and South Western; and he, together with Barr of the Caledonian, kept the flags of the old companies flying in Scotland.

On the Caledonian lines north of Glasgow and Edinburgh pre-grouping engines reigned supreme except on those three double-home compound turns from Carlisle. There were, of course, the twenty additional 60 class 4–6–0s built in 1925–6, some of which worked on passenger trains between Glasgow (Buchanan

49. The second of the Pickersgill three-cylinder 4–6–0s, now in the black livery, at Polmadie shed in 1928: engine no. 14801, originally CR no. 957.

St) and Perth; but they were not impressive engines in their work and, despite their massive frame strength and a good steaming boiler, they took rear-end banking assistance out of Buchanan Street up to Robroyston, and from Stirling up the Dunblane bank. Of the ex-Caledonian 4–4–0s of Class 3 capacity, the McIntosh Superheaters of the Dunalastair IV series always seemed to have the edge on the Pickersgills, and when in later years I made some footplate runs on the latter I found them very unimpressive. There was an afternoon train northward from Perth that was often worked by a 4–6–0, to provide power for the heavy 5.35 pm up from Aberdeen. Perth shed usually put on a Pickersgill, but occasionally one of the beautiful McIntosh 4–6–0s would turn up. There were two of the famous Cardeans at Perth in the early grouping years, then numbered 14753 and 14754, together with old no. 49, one of the two original 6 ft 6 ins type. She was a flyer in very truth, and would leave anything except a compound standing!

When I went north again in 1928, there was evidence of change on every hand. First of all an economy drive had decreed that all engines except a very few express passenger types should be painted plain black. North of Glasgow and Edinburgh this meant everything,

78

H. C. Casserley

50. At Glasgow St Enoch: one of the smaller-wheeled Manson 4–4–0s of the G&SWR, no. 14212, on a Clyde coast train. This engine is also carrying a Caledonian-type semaphore route indicator over the left-hand buffer.

except those three double-home compounds working from Carlisle to Aberdeen. On the Highland the effect was depressing beyond measure. Gone at a stroke was all the old pride of turnout. Many engines were positively filthy and the only attempt at cleaning seemed to be where the cab sides had been given a perfunctory rub in order to reveal the number! A small proportion of the engines were still in red, but these were looking shabby for the most part. It was hard to believe that such a deterioration could have taken place in twelve months. The

train working was as vigorous as ever, but photogenically most of the engines were depressing to see.

There was, however, one notable addition to the motive power stud. The six large 4–6–0 engines of 1915, originally intended to be the River class, were all in regular service on the Highland. At the time this was explained by the facile statement that the underline bridges that had precluded their use originally had been strengthened; but this was not the case at all. Their designer, F. G. Smith, was one of the foremost thinkers of the day on the finer points of locomotive design, and he had so arranged the dynamic balancing of these engines, so that although they had a considerably heavier dead

51. Aberdeen–Euston express passing Symington hauled by Midland compound 4–4–0 no. 921.

load on their coupled axles than Peter Drummond's Castles, the dynamic augment, or hammer-blow was no more. Had he been as good a diplomatist as he was a mechanical engineer he, and not Stanier, might have been Chief Mechanical Engineer of the LMS. But he had already crossed swords with the Civil Engineer of the Highland, Alexander Newlands, and the manner in which the first two engines of the River class arrived at Perth, without any formal notice, or consultation was enough to set the heather on fire. Newlands forbade their use, on the grounds of axle loading, and Smith having produced engines that could not be used was forced to resign. In the

1920s, the deliberations of the Bridge Stress Committee revealed that the Rivers could safely be used on the Highland line – in fact, their effect on the track was far less severe than that of the Clans, which Newlands accepted, because they had a lower dead loading on their coupled axles!

The Rivers were grand engines. It has always been a mystery to me why they were so little appreciated on the Caledonian. They were bought at a time when there was a desperate shortage of powerful engines, but one feels that the proud hierarchy of St Rollox looked on them as so many alien tools and never took the trouble to study the design or analyse their performance. Instead St Rollox went their own

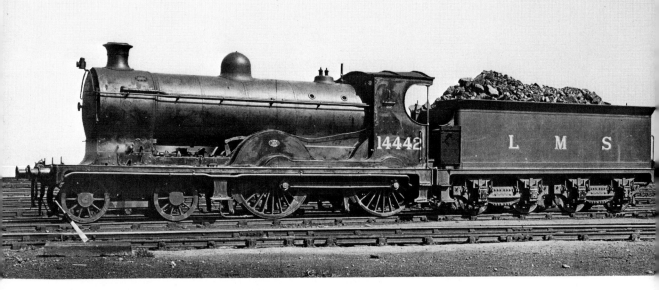

52. Ex-Caledonian superheated 'Dunalastair IV' 4–4–0
no. 14442 in plain black livery: note the huge double-bogie
tender.

way, or the ways into which Pickersgill led
them, and produced the sluggish, badly designed 60 class 4–6–0s. St Rollox were not
averse to carrying out indicator trials; one
would not have needed a dynamometer car, and
it would very quickly have been discovered that
they had in the Rivers the finest express
passenger engines that ever ran the rails in
Scotland in pre-grouping times. Despite all
the legendary exploits of that greatly loved
Caledonian 4–6–0, 'Cardean', she would not
have been able to hold a candle to the Rivers. On
the Highland, in 1928, they were terrific! Most
of them were still painted red, but in their
menial duties on the Caledonian they had
become rather grubby. When the Highland
cleaners got to work on them they assumed a
dark purple shade.

In the years now under review the Royal
Scots had not yet begun to work north of
Glasgow. The Highland and the Aberdeen

trains still changed engines at Carlisle, and were
taken forward by Kingmoor compounds, often
in pairs. With the batch of compounds numbered from 900 upwards stationed at Polmadie
the class had virtually taken over, south of
Glasgow, and equally on the G&SW route. On
the latter, despite the fervent partisanship of the
local men, one and all violently antagonistic to
the Caledonian, it cannot be said that they had
been very well served for main line motive
power in the twenty years prior to grouping.
James Manson's 4–6–0s, well designed thermo-
dynamically and economical in their running,
were not altogether sound structurally; there
were frame troubles and the cylinders worked
loose, and in any event drivers on what was
known colloquially as 'The Long Road' – as
distinct from the lines to the Clyde coast –
handled their engines on a fairly light rein. They
rarely did much in the way of hard pounding
uphill; and as the Manson 4–6–0s could run very
freely they let them go downhill, frequently
exceeding 80 mph. When Manson retired and

81

53. Red engines linger on the Highland: one of the Jones 'Loch' class 4–4–0s rebuilt with 'Dunalastair' type boiler: no. 14390, 'Loch Fannich'.

was succeeded by Peter Drummond the older engines were left alone, as the other Drummond brother did when he went to the London and South Western, and the new incumbent got on with his own ideas. But the coming of war in 1914 postponed the introduction of what was to have been Peter Drummond's greatest work, a big 4-cylinder 4–6–0; and he died in 1918 leaving the 'big engine' situation unchanged on the G&SWR. Robert Whitelegg who succeeded him could do no more than patch up the ageing 4–6–0s, and when grouping came Kilmarnock could not put up much of a show against the massed strength of St Rollox.

In other respects, however, the strong individuality of the Glasgow and South Western

Railway persisted for many years. When the Westinghouse Brake and Signal Company secured the contract for the resignalling of St Enoch station, Glasgow, in 1930, and I was sent north to obtain the necessary site data for the design of the point mechanisms and the signal mountings, I became associated with two divisional engineers whose fathers had been chief officers of the G&SWR, William Melville, Chief Engineer, and W. Bryson, Signal and Telegraph Superintendent. Their sons were strong and picturesque characters, with no exaggerated respect for their new-found and distant overlords in England. Recalling the trouble we had with Alexander Newlands over the switch extension pieces for the point mechanisms at Manchester, I was surprised to see new British standard switches drilled with

54. One of the splendid 'River' class 4–6–0s, banned from the Highland in 1915 but reinstated in 1928: no. 14759 at Blair Atholl.

extra holes to suit a temporary electrical device. When, in all deference, I mentioned to Johnny Melville the trouble we had experienced, and how we had been forbidden to drill any holes, he gave me an old fashioned look and said: 'Well, Euston's a hell of a long way away!' From the outset we had the readiest and most cordial co-operation at St Enoch, but ironically enough, in 1932 he was appointed Permanent Way Assistant at Euston, and five years later became Senior Assistant (Permanent Way) to the Chief Engineer, based at St Pancras!

No reference to the contribution the Scottish companies made to the general well-being of the LMS would be complete without a mention of the systems of single line working. When he was Locomotive Superintendent of the Great North of Scotland Railway, before his appointment to the G&SWR, James Manson had in 1890 designed his celebrated system of mechanical exchange of single line tablets, enabling this operation to be carried out at practically the maximum speed of running. It was adopted also by the Highland Railway and installed throughout the system. It worked so well that the passing loops, aided by the excellent track layouts, could be taken at speeds up to 60 mph.

It was also used on all the single-line broad gauge sections of the Belfast and Northern Counties Railway. It was not, however, used on the single-line sections of the G&SWR particularly that between Girvan and Challoch Junction, where the main line from Ayr joined the Portpatrick and Wigtownshire line from Dumfries to Stranraer. On the G&SWR the single line sections were equipped with an apparatus designed by the elder Bryson, to meet a disadvantage of the Manson apparatus, namely that it could not be used on an engine that was running tender first.

A notable feature of the Scottish railway scene in the early years of grouping was the profound change in the type of coaching stock to be found on the more local train services. On the Highland in particular, trains running between Perth and Inverness (including through sections from Glasgow and Edinburgh as well as from English stations) were mostly composed of corridor stock; but the continuation runs, to Wick and Thurso and also to Kyle of Lochalsh were, in Highland Railway days, made up of the distinctly primitive non-corridor and often non-bogie coaches. The local populace took such mode of travel as normal; indeed some old passengers regarded the coming of amenities as

rather indecent. I remember one taciturn old islesman, when the morning train from Inverness drew into Achnasheen abreast of the restaurant car on the corresponding up train saying: 'Ay, there's some swanky trains going to Kyle now.' I am afraid we folks from the south did not regard them as anything very special, because we recognised them as made up of superannuated Midland and North Western stock!

One old Highlander would have invoked the wrath of the Gods upon us, when the call came to take our seats for lunch. 'You with your eating and drinking in a railway train', he exclaimed, 'it is a wonder the mountains do not fall down and crush you all!' Although it would have been an experience I am glad there were corridor coaches, if not necessarily restaurant cars, when I first travelled on the Kyle and Farther North trains. Things must have been a bit grim on these long drawn out journeys, when, as the late R. E. Charlewood once expressed it; intermediate stops were made at 'A', 'B' and 'C' for the engine to take water and the passengers to make it! The dining cars that I recall working north of Inverness in those early grouping years were mostly of Midland origin.

10
A Time of Vital Changes

The skill that Sir Josiah Stamp brought to bear upon the management of the LMS in his choice of senior executives was an outstanding feature of his chairmanship. One choice among the original four Vice-Presidents taking office from January 1927 was that of R. W. Reid, the former Carriage and Wagon Superintendent, and his unexpected and untimely death only two years later, at the early age of forty-four, left a gap that there was some difficulty in filling. He was a son of W. P. Reid, formerly Locomotive Superintendent of the North British Railway, and well known to locomotive enthusiasts by his beautiful Atlantic engines with their fine Scottish names, and his Scott and Glen class 4–4–0s. His son, Robert Whyte, had entered the service of the Midland Railway in 1909 as Works Assistant in the Carriage and Wagon Department, and no more than seven years later, at the early age of thirty-one, he was appointed Works Manager. He had already caught the eye of Sir Guy Granet, and in 1919 when the veteran chief of the department, David Bain, retired Reid became Carriage and Wagon Superintendent of the Midland Railway. When no more than eight years later, at the still early age of forty-two he was appointed Vice-President, for Works and Ancillary Undertakings, such distinguished engineers as Sir Henry Fowler, and Alexander Newlands re-

ported to him. Many years later when visiting the Montreal Locomotive Works I had the pleasure of meeting his son, A. R. M. Reid, who was then manager of the Heat Transfer Products Group of that great organisation.

Reid's death led to reconsideration of the top-management structure of the LMS, particularly towards the vital matter of research. Hitherto this had been done on a more or less hand-to-mouth basis, by the engineering departments concerned, as and when problems arose, as in the case of the piston-valve troubles on the Royal Scot class locomotives. But Stamp and Granet felt that the time had come for research to be put on a more forward-looking basis, to be overseen directly at Vice-President level; and in meeting the need for a replacement for Reid, the view developed that this particular Vice-President, necessarily to be a man of the highest technical and scientific qualifications, and achievement, should also embrace research. In seeking around Granet lighted upon his own *alma mater*, Balliol College, Oxford, and the choice fell upon Sir Harold Hartley, Fellow and Tutor of the College since 1901, who had so brilliant a subsequent career in both science and industry as to gain him Fellowship of the Royal Society. He took up office as a Vice-President of the LMS in January 1930, with the additional title of Director of Scientific Research.

55. The last throw of Midlandisation: the standard '2P' 4–4–0, representing a slightly modernised version of the Midland rebuilt 7 ft 4–4–0, and with 6 ft 9 in. coupled wheels.

His experience up to that time had been entirely outside railways, mainly to do with the chemical and gas industries, and it was considered that at first he would need a senior assistant, to advise, more particularly on mechanical engineering matters. Stamp doubtless had in mind the thorny matter of the succession in the Chief Mechanical Engineer's department. The fires of partisanship between Crewe and Derby continued to smoulder, and in 1930 H. P. M. Beames had every reason to hope that he would be the successor to Sir Henry Fowler. Stamp had come to the conclusion that such an appointment would be disastrous, not so much in the nature or quality of new locomotive

designs that would result, because Beames, in his re-organisation of Crewe Works had shown himself to be a first-rate mechanical engineer, supremely aware of the needs of the modern railway. It was in the antagonisms that the imposition of neo-Crewe practice generally that the danger would arise. The transition, however it was achieved, could not be done quickly, and Stamp became convinced that the only way to secure real cohesion in the locomotive department was to bring in a complete outsider.

The need of Sir Harold Hartley for some high-level assistance in his early days gave an opportunity to detach Sir Henry Fowler. Many of his staff felt that however suitable he undoubtedly was for the job of Assistant to the Vice-President it was a case of side-tracking not in keeping with the dignity of his previous high office. They felt he should have retired. But that

56. The LMS version of the LNWR 'G2' 0–8–0 introduced in 1929. One hundred were built at Crewe.

was not in the nature of Sir Henry Fowler. He had, in 1926, accepted the undoubted affront to his position, when he was instructed to stop work on his compound Pacific, test a Great Western Castle, and then to get fifty new 3-cylinder 4–6–0s built in a shipwreck hurry. So also, in 1931, he seems to have been happy enough to move sideways, as it were, into whole-time research. When R. W. Reid had been made a Vice-President in 1927 his former post of Carriage and Wagon Engineer had passed to E. J. H. Lemon, and the capacity of the latter for sound organisation, and his relatively neutral background led to his being appointed Chief Mechanical Engineer in succession to Fowler. His appointment was more than this. On both the London and North Western and on the Midland Railways the Carriage and Wagon Department had been separate and independent of that dealing with locomotives, and this situation had remained in the early years of the LMS. In this respect it differed from the practice of the other three 'group' railways, on all of which the Chief Mechanical Engineer included carriages and wagons in his charge. In 1931 Lemon also obtained total supervision though, as on the Southern and the LNER, no responsibility for locomotive running.

Another important top-level appointment, as from January 1930, was that of W. V. Wood to be Vice-President in charge of Finance and Service Departments. His railway career had begun in 1898 on the Belfast and Northern Counties Railway, but on the formation of the Ministry of Transport in 1919 he was transferred to London as Director of Transport

87

57. A variant of the popular and successful Horwich 2–6–0, having the Lentz rotary cam poppet valve gear.

(Accounting). In 1924 he returned to the railway service on the LMS. He was later to represent the LMS on the wartime Railway Executive Committee and after the tragic death of Lord Stamp, as he had by then become, in 1941, he became President of the Executive of the LMS.

A change in engineering organisation of considerable note had taken place in the previous May, and was one of the last innovations for which R. W. Reid was responsible before his death. Until then supervision of the Signalling and Telegraph works of the company had been exercised by the Chief Civil Engineer and by the Electrical Engineer respectively, as on the Southern and London and North Eastern Railways. But as from May 1929 it was decided that these works should be managed by a combined department under an officer of such seniority as to report direct to the Vice-President for Works and Ancillary equipment. The signalling and telegraph activity was thus put on an equivalent status to that of the Chief Civil Engineer, and of the Chief Mechanical Engineer. The step was widely welcomed in the signalling profession, because of the evidence it provided of the grow-

ing awareness in top railway management of the importance of signalling and telecommunications towards the efficient handling of modern traffic. None of the divisional signal engineers, reporting to the respective civil engineers was of sufficient stature to fulfil this new office and the choice fell upon A. F. Bound, previously Signal Engineer of the Southern Area of the LNER. He was a man of long and varied experience having served a premium apprenticeship in the locomotive department of the LB&SCR at Brighton, under R. J. Billinton, from 1894 to 1898. It was not until 1902 that he had his first experience of signalling, and then as an outside assistant for the British Pneumatic Railway Signal Co. A year later he joined the Great Central Railway, and became Signal Superintendent three years later.

He came to play a prominent part in the proceedings of the Institution of Railway Signal Engineers, and was regarded as one of the most forward looking of its members. When the epoch-marking 'Three Position Signal Committee' of that Institution was set up in March 1922 he was appointed Chairman, and presided over deliberations lasting more than two years, during which the code of multiple-aspect colour

58. The end of an era: the last ex-Furness Railway heavy mineral 0–6–0 of Pettigrew's design to retain the original boiler.

light signalling which later became standard on the railways of Great Britain was hammered out to an almost unanimous acceptance. He was elected President of the Institution of Railway Signal Engineers in 1924, at about the same time as he was appointed Signal Engineer of the Southern Area of the LNER after his old company, the Great Central, had become a constituent of that group. On the LNER he had, in accordance with ruling practice, been responsible to the Civil Engineer of the Southern Area. His appointment to very high office on the LMS was naturally regarded as of outstanding importance. The names of his principal assistant, and of the four divisional signal engineers, appointed later in 1929 and their former railways, were:

Principal Assistant: Lt-Col P. D. Michod (LNWR)
Divisional Engineer, Crewe: H. E. Morgan (Midland)
Divisional Engineer, London: A. Oldham (LNWR)
Divisional Engineer, Manchester: W. R. Jones (LNWR)
Divisional Engineer, Scotland: A. S. Hampton (Caledonian)

Reverting to locomotive matters a remarkable experimental design for which Sir Henry Fowler was responsible, in collaboration with the Superheater Co. Ltd, and built in Glasgow at the works of the North British Locomotive Co. Ltd, was the double-pressure three-cylinder compound 4–6–0, on the Royal Scot chassis, but with a boiler of the Schmidt high pressure type consisting of three distinct systems, or boilers, each carrying a different pressure. That carrying

89

59. LNWR types still active: one of the Bowen Cooke superheater 4–6–2 tanks, used for banking and local duties, leaving Oxenholme on a local train for Carlisle, consisting of ex-Midland stock. The engine is no. 6960.

the highest pressure was in the form of a closed circuit, consisting of a number of pipes that formed the sides, roof and back end of the firebox. This closed circuit was initially filled to a pre-determined level with pure water, and this latter was the medium by means of which heat was transmitted from the firebox to the evaporating elements in the high pressure drum. It was from this latter that steam at the very high pressure of 900 lbs per sq. in. was supplied to the high-pressure cylinder of the locomotive.

The low-pressure boiler, working at the normal Royal Scot pressure of 250 lb per sq. in., was of the ordinary locomotive type, with its barrel immediately in rear of the smokebox. Steam exhausted from the high pressure cylinder entered a mixing chamber where it was met by low pressure steam at 250 lb per sq. in. from the low pressure boiler. It was not compound working in the normal sense because steam

60. As late as 1929, ex-LNWR engines were still on the two-hour Birmingham expresses, as shown here, with superheated 'Precursor' class 4–4–0 no. 5308, 'Simoom', dating from 1904.

exhausted from the high pressure cylinder, after expansion, was reinforced by steam generated at the lower pressure. This highly unorthodox conception, based upon an experimental loco-motive that was reported to have run satis-factorily on one of the Continental railways, was Fowler's last bow in the world of loco-motives. It showed that his predilection for compounds still remained; but whether it would have proved more economical than a Royal Scot was not to be known. The locomotive never ran in revenue earning service; its trials in Scotland were suspended and never recommenced after a disastrous accident while running through Carstairs station. The bursting of a superheater tube caused a terrible blow-back of steam and part of the fire killed one of the crew. In retrospect one is bound to admit it was unlikely that such an unorthodox, complicated and ex-pensive machine would ever have been accept-able for ordinary day to day traffic.

What proved to be the last incident in the sustained rivalry between Derby and Crewe locomotive works came at the end of 1930. The Claughton class engines with the enlarged boilers, and particularly the batch that retained the original valve gear but had piston valves with solid heads and six narrow rings, had proved so successful and so economical in fuel consumption that Derby felt they had to produce their version of a 5X 4–6–0. So an ingenious hybrid was worked out, using the Royal Scot type of chassis and cylinder arrangements and the enlarged Claughton boiler. The first two engines of the new series, nos 5902 and 5971, were actually rebuilds of Claughtons adapting the original frames and using the standard Crewe bogie. But the new cylinder layout and dimensions were the same as the Royal Scots (18 ins diameter by 26 ins stroke) and the nominal tractive effort was less in proportion to the reduced boiler pressure of 200, instead of 250 lb per sq. in. The rebuilding of the first two engines of the series was done at Derby.

Engine no. 5971 when newly rebuilt was stationed at Leeds, Midland shed, and working on the Carlisle road came into the limelight via 'British locomotive practice and performance' in the *Railway Magazine*. None of her early work, thus publicised, was of the best standards then being maintained by the batch of unaltered Claughtons then allocated to that route; but, of course, logs compiled by anyone travelling passenger cannot tell the whole story, and the performance of this engine, and of no. 5902 allocated to the LNW section was such that further conversions – or rather replacements – were authorised. The fifteen engines outshopped from Crewe in 1932 were virtually new, except for using a few, non-vital parts. But they took the numbers of the Claughtons they replaced, and accountancy-wise, no doubt, they were classed as rebuilds. In general service, particularly on the Manchester and Wolverhampton trains to and from Euston, they quickly acquired an excellent reputation; and while they did not show an appreciably lower basic coal consumption than the enlarged Claughtons that retained four cylinders their repair costs were considerably lower, and that was what mattered. Their history, however, belongs to the second phase of the LMS saga, and must be deferred until the second volume.

At the beginning of the 1930s, therefore, the LMS had survived its often-traumatic formative years and with Stamp at the helm was poised ready for the great developments of the next ten years, achieved, nevertheless, against a background that was often sombre, in the midst of industrial depression, and later against the menacing threat of a second world war.

Index